Melvin Gorham's Interpretation

of

Richard Wagner's

THE VALKYRIE

Together with
The Morality of the
Early Northern Europeans

by

John Harland

Published by

SOVEREIGN PRESS
326 Harris Road
Rochester, WA 98579

Revised Edition

ISBN 0-914752-24-3

Library of Congress Catalog Card Number 86-63393

Manufactured in the United States of America

To Evelyn

Foreword

Wagner's Ring operas, drawing on Northern European mythology of prehistory age, are built upon the archetypal symbols of the subconscious. Present attention to these greatest musical dramas of all time has shown some tendency toward reducing the symbols to abstractions. This work moves in the opposite direction — toward bringing the symbols into waking consciousness.

The basic elements of the events depicted in the Ring operas are repeated in all times under widely varying circumstances. This interpretation is set in the first half of the twenty-first century to permit full freedom in translating the subconscious symbols into their present day counterparts. The concept of "nation" might otherwise be an obstacle. The subconscious, of course, can have no symbol for nation other than a living organism — a giant creature, man-like when considered as something with which communication is possible; dragon-like when looked upon as a thing to be fought. The mythology of the Northern Europeans was concerned with the undesirable aspects of the nations pressing in upon them from the Mediterranean shores. Nations, per se, were to them essentially undesirable, even as they became to the American Indians. The reverse concept, instilled in every school child in the current world, creates an understandable tendency *away from* letting the subconscious symbols of the Ring operas come up and find their counterparts in waking consciousness. The viewpoint of the prehistory Northern Europeans is more closely approached here by depicting the "nations", not as the institutions known with reverence, but as police-states controlled by gangsters with a political facade — as might happen after atomic wars had reduced the metropolitan world to a few cities too minor to have been prime targets.

Such is the condition set forth in *The Curse of the Ring,* my narrative interpretation of *The Rhinegold,* which forms the background for *The Valkyrie*. After the first atomic wars two "giants", two gangster controlled police-states, came into existence — FASOLT (Federated American Society of Latin Territories) and FAFNER, a similar police-state claiming the entire eastern hemisphere.

Wotan was the leader of an embryonic organization of free people, dedicated to individual sovereignty and calling themselves

7

sovereigns. He propagandized against the police-states by calling them teras (monsters) instead of nations, calling their unthinking components zombis or segments (sometimes terasegments) instead of citizens, and calling their outcasts which they banished to the wilds, dwarfs, because their life as segments had given them small, distorted souls.

Propaganda, or ideological warfare, aimed at keeping the people of the police-states brainwashed and attracting the people still living in the wilds, was a major activity. The best television program each year received an award of the highly coveted Ring (comparable to the movies' Oscar of the present day). FASOLT and FAFNER constantly competed for a hypothetical supreme Ring which was not actually awarded but was recognized in symbol.

FASOLT modelled a television program on Wotan's daring and exploits as a warrior-leader, and tried to adapt his ideals of freedom as propaganda against its rival FAFNER. Instead of hurting FAFNER, the program, called "Men Like Gods", had the effect of raising the sovereigns led by Wotan to a world power. Seeing the efficacy of television, Wotan sought a world-wide television program of his own. He also bargained with FAFNER and FASOLT jointly, to build Valhalla, an impressive city for the "Men Like Gods". His plan was that the sovereigns could use Valhalla as a symbol to hold their own followers and even to attract those who still looked upon them with distaste as the "wildspeople".

Logi, Wotan's attorney who had defected from FAFNER, worked in good faith on the contract for building Valhalla but the final result was a treaty prohibiting Wotan from further political activity in most of the areas of the world.

Now, twenty-five years since the events described in *The Curse of the Ring,* the only actively functioning "nation" left in the world is the police-state FAFNER. Wotan and the "gods" still have their great city, Valhalla. Also they have some planes, including even some bombing planes under command of Donner, but they are bound by treaties not to use the bombers unless FAFNER breaks treaty first.

Wagner's great operas are such consummate works of art that, except for translation of the subconscious archetypes, no significant change is conceivable. This work, of course, is intended only as an examination of one small facet of the finely-cut, manyfaceted jewel that is Wagner's great work.

Melvin Gorham

THE VALKYRIE
A Play in Three Acts

Based upon Richard Wagner's THE VALKYRIE

CHARACTERS

MALE — 3

SIEGMUND, *a young man of the forest*
HUNDING, *a policeman, an official of the police-state*
WOTAN, *a mature warrior-leader*

FEMALE — 11

LINDA, *wife of Hunding, lover of Siegmund*
BRUNNHILDE, *Chief of the Valkyries*
FRICKA, *wife of Wotan*
VALKYRIES, *plane-pilots of battle rescue service — 8*

MALE OR FEMALE

Radio technicians, 2 or more, optional, non-speaking characters

ACT ONE

The room has some tasteless pretention toward luxury but no distinctive theme. The furniture and decorations are unrelated pieces, random remainders from those once produced in mass quantities to ride momentary fads; they could be valued only because their materials and gloss are reminiscent of the past industrial era. A thief with no taste might have assembled the room's furniture, or a policeman. A certificate of appointment conspicuously displayed on one wall indicates that this is the home of the area's chief of police. Only the fire burning in the fireplace gives meaning and warmth to the room.

A young man whose head and hair are matted with dried blood and who moves as if in pain, but still with the quiet motions of a hunting or hunted animal, slips quickly through the room's outer door and closes it soundlessly behind him. His leather clothes and movements show that he does not belong where he finds himself. He uses his last energy to look through the inner door for occupants and finding none half lies down, half collapses, in front of the fireplace and immediately loses consciousness.

No one in the house would have heard him enter. No one would have been alerted. But he was too tired for full caution and the house does have another occupant.

A young woman comes from the inner door with a bowl of water and a few scrawny flowers. Good breeding has given her a heritage of beauty but there is no happiness left in her face. She moves not as the mistress of the house but as its unwilling caretaker. Only for the flowers does she have a glance of more than perfunctory attention. She regards each of the scrawny little things with affection, picks off the withered leaves and places the battered blossoms in the bowl of water she has set in the middle of the table. Without looking around to see how the arrangement fits the room, she looks at the flowers as if they were the whole of her world at the moment. They are not much; they could be a focus for her attention only because all other moments must stretch behind and ahead in utter greyness. She looks at them as a prisoner long in confinement might look upon a moth that had come through the window bars to crawl on the grey stone walls of his cell — something of small in-

terest in otherwise unbroken monotony. She dips one of the flowers fully into the water as if it looked especially thirsty to her and resets it in its place. Then, without glancing around the room, she leaves by the door she had entered.

She returns with her arms filled with firewood and then, only because the sleeping man is directly in her path, she sees him. She is young but something already has overlaid her fine breeding with dullness; she is surprised but she no longer has the capacity for being startled — for quick reaction, or for wonder. Like a dull beast of burden she stops when confronted by the obstacle, looks at the situation, goes around the man and puts the wood by the fire as she had intended. Only then does she turn to examine the intruder with care. She looks at his leather clothes with only a little more wonder and interest than the flowers had inspired. She looks at the handsome young face, still trembling even in sleep with the efforts that caused its exhaustion, and her hands move of themselves as if they would touch and soothe him, even though the mind that should be directing them has been dulled to all emotion. She restrains her hands but somewhere deep within her a spark of life has awakened.

She leaves the room again, returns with a basin and a sponge, kneels by the unconscious man and gently bathes the wound on his head. Her touch is so gentle that at first he sleeps undistrubed. He then awakens with the instantaneous alertness and readiness for action that characterizes a wild animal. Seeing in a quick scanning look that only the girl is in the room, he freezes in the ready-for-action position he had instantly assumed and looks to see what she is doing. The basin of liquid catches his attention. He reacts with the involuntary compulsion of a very thirsty man seeing the object of his desire and starts to take the basin and drink from it.

SIEGMUND. Water.

LINDA. Don't drink that. It's medicated. I'll get you some water. *(She exits and returns with a clay mug of water and he drinks it all.)*

(They look at each other a long time, each waiting for the other's next action.)

LINDA. *(Her tone evidences a slowly returning capacity for wonder.)* You are from the wilds.

SIEGMUND. *(does not confirm; he knows no confirmation but his appearance is necessary. He continues looking at her. Her superficial appearance is that of all establishment people but the understanding in her eyes is a puzzle.)* And who are you? Who are you that you don't run screaming? Who are you that you help a man of my appearance when you find me on your hearth?

LINDA. I am Linda, given as wife to Hunding, FAFNER's chief

of police for this area. Maybe I can help if you need help.

SIEGMUND. Hunding! *(The word explodes from him as a bitter laugh.)* This is Hunding's house? I get help and hospitality in the house of the area's chief of police! What sport with me can fate now plan?

LINDA. I'd like to help you. I'll get you some food. *(She takes the basin and the water mug, hurries out and soon returns with a pitcher and two mugs.)* I have food such as comes from the wilds. I can eat synthetics but I don't like them. This has alcohol, honey, eggs, and milk. Would you like it?

SIEGMUND. *(notes the two mugs.)* If you drink with me. *(Linda fills the two mugs, sips hers while he drinks deeply. He then gets to his feet and makes ready to go. She pours him another mug and offers it. He looks at her, still puzzled, then takes the mug, drains it, and hands it back.)*

SIEGMUND. Your kindness, even more than the much needed food and drink, has given me strength. Now I must go before my bad fortune rubs off on you.

LINDA. Do you need a place to hide? Are you being followed?

SIEGMUND. Only by bad luck, as far as I know, but I don't want it to follow me here and find you. *(He stands looking at her; he finds it difficult to break away.)* Something in your eyes feeds a deep hunger in me — but I must go. *(He crosses the room and starts to open the door.)*

LINDA. Don't leave. You can bring no more bad fortune here. Bad fortune lives here always — in full measure. This is its home.

SIEGMUND. *(is easily persuaded to stay; he studies her with more interest.)* Hunding is my foremost enemy and I his. If he is also your enemy I can not do better than meet him here. *(His eyes question hers while he stands with his hand on the door.)*

(For answer Linda takes his hand from the door and draws him back into the room. As they stand searching each other's eyes in silence as animals search each other for breed-meaning and attitude, there is a sound of someone outside. Linda goes to the door and opens it for her husband.)

(Hunding is the prototype of all who find the fullest expression of their nature as policemen. He wears a dark cloth uniform and a saber. Seeing the intruder, Siegmund, he stops with the dramatic attitude of offended authority, the pose that is his lifeblood, and fixes on Linda a hard glance that demands explanation.)

LINDA. I found him asleep on the hearth, hurt and exhausted.

HUNDING. And — instead of calling for someone to deal with the intruder, you welcomed him.

LINDA. I did. *(Her tone is that of one who has been inter-*

rogated endlessly, but there is a faint new note of defiance that does not escape Hunding. He bristles even more.)

SIEGMUND. She was kind. She let me rest and gave me a drink. Is that a crime to the Commander of Police?

HUNDING. My house is the entertainment center for all Nibelung. We have all sorts of riffraff as guests. *(He seems pleased with his witicism and expansive in appreciation of himself.)* There seems to be none for dinner tonight. We might as well have you.

(Hunding looks at Linda with a smug self-satisfaction that relishes what he thinks of as subtlety and cleverness in applying the insolence of office. Without a further word Linda begins to prepare the table for dinner. Siegmund stands with silent readiness and watches the situation. He takes renewed strength from time to time by drinking in Linda's returning beauty. She feeds the return of that beauty by stolen glances at him.)

HUNDING. *(studies Linda and Siegmund closely, and observes the similarity of breeding and the understanding that clearly exists between them.)* Obviously you are from the wilds and, like a wild animal, you doubtless have not acquired the taste for synthetic foods as have proper men. Then you have come to the right place. My wife is a low-born woman of the wilds, and still retains her taste for organic foods. Since she will eat them in secret, anyway, I let her eat them at the table like a human being. Perhaps she came from your own area? You seem to have traveled far?

SIEGMUND. All my life I have traveled, never remaining long anywhere. What place I could call home would be hard to say. I've never before seen a great city and I slipped in when none were watching to get a first hand look at the wonders. More I would like to see and know.

(Hunding motions him to sit. Siegmund obeys and he and Hunding sit and eat while Linda waits on the table. Hunding feels a pompous relish for a host's role; he is almost expansive.)

HUNDING. The great cities are now mostly tales of the past. There is one still in FAFNER that is the center of world government. It is the only real city now left in the world. I answer to the top authorities there, and govern all Nibelung from here. This little city grows ever smaller, as do all since the last atomic war. But we try to retain some semblance of civilization. ... And you, a roving animal, for what purpose do you live, if any? *(Siegmund ponders how he will answer the surprising question and is silent in thought so long Hunding prods him.)* If you think I could see no reason for your existence, tell your story to my wife. She has strange taste in companions. See how eagerly she hangs on your words.

LINDA. I would be happy to hear.

16

SIEGMUND. *(settles back as if preparing to tell a long story.)* I barely remember my father but I know he lived a free man and died a free man. He always remembered Wotan's promise that someday a leader would arise. He encouraged the good men of Nibelung to remain faithful to their ideals of freedom. But there was the great war and no leader came.

HUNDING. *(interrupting)* None will ever come. Forget it.

SIEGMUND. *(waits for Hunding to say more, then continues.)* When I was a very small boy I remember the police as horsemen with long swords. Later I learned that they were constantly raiding the villages on the pretense of collecting the high taxes no one could pay. They demanded to be quartered in our houses and then made free with the women. My father roused our village to resist. Every man in the village was killed, the village was burned, most of the women were killed, and a few who were young and pretty were carried away. My most vivid early memory is of my mother lying dead in a pool of blood. Then I was led through the burning town by my older brother. He was maybe nine years old and I five. Somehow we escaped into the woods. My brother had learned to hunt with my father and we lived alone in the woods for years. I grew up and learned to take care of myself. *(Although he and Hunding are sitting at the table and Linda is acting as waitress his words have been for her. He now focuses on Hunding.)* That is my story, a sort you doubtless know well from another viewpoint.

HUNDING. Terrible and wild is your story, my hardy guest. Animals you must be to survive in the woods even as children. Yes, I have had my part in such raids. That was when I was a young officer not yet tied down with a chief's duties. But I was more thorough. If it had been my job to make an example of your village, I would not have you as my guest tonight.

LINDA. Tell us further, stranger. How did you come to know the big world, as your speech and knowledge of things other than the forest shows you do?

SIEGMUND. My brother and I were lonely and sought our kind. We began to hang around the villages. When my brother was almost a man he developed a fondness for a young hunter his age. We went with him to live in the village. There still, as my brother had remembered from his childhood, were the overbearing officials. The police still caused some to abandon their homes for a life in the forest and some to resist, even when they knew resistance would only result in their slaughter.

HUNDING. You people never learn. *(Siegmund again waits for Hunding to say more.)*

LINDA. Please go on stranger.

17

SIEGMUND. We had not been in the village long when a draft call came for young men to join the very police that was guilty of the atrocities against them. My brother was among those drafted. No one could believe that such things could be. But there was a rumor that the village was to be made self-governing, that the draftees were to be made police in our own village and would be able to improve conditions. So they gathered in the town square to listen. They were still suspicious and all had knives. They were told of the ease and rewards of the life, and bribes were offered to those who went willingly. While the talks were in progress more police came in and surrounded the square. Then when no one would accept bribes the police tried to carry all off by force. Their strength was little but their courage was great and, at the agreed signal, they all fought. Mere boys, surrounded and outnumbered ten to one by grown men on horseback, they fought for a brief moment. They were butchered to the last one like cattle and the horsemen made a point of riding over their bloody bodies.

(Siegmund has been watching Hunding closely as he talked, and glancing at Linda, he sees that she, too, is watching Hunding anxiously. She goes to a stand at the back of the room and mixes drinks, secretly dropping something into one intended for Hunding. While at the stand she also cuts the cord of the telephone. Meanwhile Hunding is answering Siegmund.)

HUNDING. Your lot is very grievous when looked at from your viewpoint. And you are doubtless blind to any other. It seems impossible to teach you wildspeoples to cooperate like civilized beings. I suppose you identify me with the sufferings that you think are unjust. So even while you are still my guest I'd better play safe. I'll call in two or three of my men. *(He starts to leave the table for the telephone.)*

LINDA. *(interrupts him by returning with the drinks.)* Does the Commander in Chief of all Nibelung police, himself armed, in his own home and the center of his own city, want to appear a coward before his subordinates? Do you really want to ask for help against one exhausted weaponless man? Wait and hear the rest of the stranger's story before deciding what to do.

HUNDING. Well, my throat is dry. I'll at least have a drink first. *(He settles down again and drinks what she has brought him.)*

LINDA. *(tries to keep the conversation going.)* Stranger, what happened then? What happened when you were alone and old enough to have some first-hand opinions of the world?

SIEGMUND. At that time I was twelve years old, almost a man in my own eyes. So I thought I'd not wait helplessly until my brother's fate became my own. I formed what I called an army, an army made up of boys like myself from the village. We left the village forever, and deep in the woods we set up our camp. I knew how to live in the forest and the other boys, too, had spent some time in the woods. We all became good hunters and were fully self-sufficient. We grew older, began to move about and gain recruits. We grew to numbers too great to hide out successfully. So we split, and grew, and split again. How many groups and how many men we now are I don't know, but we will someday find a way to unite and destroy the police. *(He notices that the drug is beginning to take effect on Hunding and tries to keep him interested a little longer.)* We give your police plenty of trouble even now. But we lose our men too. My group was completely destroyed two days ago. We were on our way here to learn something of the real might of our enemy. We passed a village where police had moved in on a local picnic. They outnumbered the townsmen present so, of course, they started a fight. We were half their number but we cut off their escape route and fought them from evening, all through the night, and half the next day. We would have killed them to the last man but in the night one must have escaped and gone for help. Hordes such as I had never seen converged on us, and unless others like me were left for dead and were not, there are none left of my band but myself.

HUNDING. *(rising)* I know well your wild blooded breed now. You leather jackets have given us nothing but trouble. Because of you the villagers, who might be taught discipline, are inspired with false hope. The false hope leads to their futile resistance and to bloodshed. If you were not fools you would understand that we must destroy you to the last man. There is nothing else to do. What civilized men revere you flout unawed. You are trying to turn civilization back to the dark ages of beasts in the jungle. I know of the fight you mention. I, myself, ordered the cavalry to it at full speed. ...And now I find the vile breed's leader sitting calmly under my roof and eating at my table. Well, you came to discover the force of the enemy. So you shall. I'll have the house surrounded in a minute. *(He starts away but, almost falling, steadies himself on a chair and continues.)* When I have a few skilled young swordsmen here you can have some kind of knife. We'll give you an opportunity to show your own great skill and courage. The administration in FAFNER is a stickler for the terms of the treaty. The treaty says: "Troops shall be used only to put down armed rebellion." We always follow the law to the letter. So you will be allowed to go to your death fighting. *(He stumbles before reaching the phone; trying to catch himself, he reaches for the side of the door and falls in the doorway.)*

LINDA. He's only drugged, not dead, but he'll sleep all night. That will give you a chance to escape. Help me put him on his bed.

(They remove Hunding and return, Siegmund first. He stands thoughtfully looking into the fire until Linda rejoins him, then tells her what he has been thinking.)

SIEGMUND. There is a legend that the right leader will have a way to know he's the right leader. It says that he will find here, in the very midst of the enemy, men of good faith, stout hearts, and strong arms — enough such men for a real army, a weapon powerful enough to defend honor and free all the people from their subjection to the police-state. I remembered the legend while coming here and I have looked for significance in everything. But I wasn't prepared for what I've actually found. It is not what I expected but it seems to mean something. Here you are, a woman in whose eyes I see response to my deepest yearnings and highest aspirations. Here you are, married to this man, and needing a defender as much as any woman I have ever known. And here am I, alone — without an army to fight the real enemy, the big one; Hunding is only a segment, scarcely more than a symbol. It looks like a hopeless situation — but, looking at you, I am convinced that somehow, someway, the legend must be true. I see in you my own breed and my own ideals, and I find you ready, ready even without my asking, to aid and defend with full understanding the things that are my life's blood and yours.

LINDA. Did you know that before I drugged Hunding.

SIEGMUND. Yes, I knew from the first. But now I make something special of it. If you, who are the symbol and substance of the things I fight for, can be found in the house that shelters also the symbol and substance of the things I fight, then there could also be men interspersed everywhere in the camp of the enemy, who are just waiting for the right time to show their colors. There would be nothing I could not do if I could call forth that army. I could not only destroy my old enemy. I could defend what is dearer to me than ever before, now that I see it all in your eyes.

LINDA. *(pauses to consider the great step she is facing. She studies Siegmund again carefully before telling him.)* I think you might be the awaited leader and I can show you the weapon you need.

SIEGMUND. Are you telling me that it does exist — and you know actual facts about it?

LINDA. The legend is entirely true. The weapon is always visible to those who have eyes to see. Hunding sleeps soundly now. But he sleeps almost as soundly when awake. There have been many guests here. Their coming flatters him greatly and he has not doubted all came to court the favor of his office.

20

SIEGMUND. You know that you need never fear harm from me. Tell me exactly how things are. Tell me in words I can understand, not the difficult symbols of legend.

LINDA. I'll tell you everything. But first I will tell you how I happen to know. Like you I was left an orphan when a child, after just such a raid as you described. For awhile I lived with good families in the villages. Then I was abducted, brought here, and sold to Hunding for his wife. The kidnapers claimed to be my legal guardians. No one believed them, of course, but everyone pretended to believe. Officially, everything was in order. I was not raped without full legal sanction. A pompous wedding was performed with all the bad taste that goes with Hunding's position. I felt like a captive animal in a cage. But even during the wedding festivities I learned that all hope was not gone. I overheard men talking sympathetically of my fate. They said then that there were enough in the government, who were appauled by incidents of the sort, to seize and overthrow it if they had the right leader. Then they talked of Wotan, and of the men who had shown themselves for his ideals at the time of his broadcasts, just before the big war. They talked with understanding and I knew they would fight if they knew how. They are still ready to fight.

SIEGMUND. If they are ready why don't they strike?

LINDA. There is only one problem, organization. The forest people are destroyed because they're scattered and without unity. Those here would like to fight on the side of the wildspeople. They know the establishment's weak points and could help plan strategy. But they can't fight alone. They lack a base of operations.

SIEGMUND. There are plenty of possible bases in the wilds.

LINDA. Yes, I know. Everyone knows. The wildspeople are faithful; they will fight and die to the last man. So the wildslands must be the base of operation and supply. Here perhaps ten out of a hundred are potential sovereigns, ten are dwarfs by breeding and temperament, and the other eighty are total zombis, nothing but ciphers. They resemble animated counter chips in elections and they give mass inertia in battle, but they simply follow "the properly constituted authority" — the side on top. If Nibelung could be taken they would cause no trouble. All Nibelung could then be a base for full operations against FAFNER. The right ten in each hundred would be faithful. The needed weapon is here for the leader who can use it.

SIEGMUND. How could I get in contact with these people?

LINDA. There's a loose fellowship; each man knows the other and they all know me. They come here to this house and, because they know I am an eternal enemy to Hunding and all he stands for, they take me into their confidence. They want to know how to live

21

with their brothers and sisters beyond the borders that separate them. I tell them about life in the wilds and I serve them organic food. Hunding thinks I do it as a novel entertainment. They are good men but — like their food — their concepts have been synthesized until they fear what they would face if they revolted, if they had to retreat to the wilds. They are afraid to trust either food or emotions or people that are organic and natural. They need a leader who is more than a planner of battles. They need a leader who can understand both the people of the wilds and those in the cities, a leader who can unite siblings who have lost their identity. Such a man has his army ready and that man will have my undying love.

SIEGMUND. Always my hand has needed only to touch a weapon for me to fight the uniformed gangsters of the police-state. But my fight has always been blind instinct, like that of the bobcat and the tormented bear. Yet deep within me a voice always cried "yes" to life when everywhere I saw only death, disappointment and despair. Now in your eyes I see the meaning of that voice within me. Your eyes show me what I've always fought *for* and your words show me a weapon to continue my fight. *(He faces her proudly.)* Your long awaited leader stands before you. From this moment I claim both weapon and woman as my own.

(Linda's involuntary motions confirm her understanding. Siegmund takes her in his arms and she joyously presses herself to him.)

LINDA. The moment you first opened your eyes and looked into mine, my heart cried out to you with joy. Everything before that moment became strange and foreign. In your eyes I saw myself as I would be.

SIEGMUND. I have often dreamed of a woman's love but it was never sudden, complete, and unexpected — never in my most fanciful dreams.

LINDA. In this short time you have become everything to me, my love, my hero, my rescuer, the champion of my ideals. You're more than that; you are my soul and being; you are my body and bone.

SIEGMUND. *(holds her still closer.)* You are my comrade in arms and lover united in one. With such a bride my blood and bone will shout with joy forever.

LINDA. *(breaks away from him with joyous laughter.)* If I am to be your comrade I must not stay in your arms. Mysterious forces like those of the legend seem to be showing us a direction, but we, ourselves, must lend a hand to our destiny.

SIEGMUND. Suddenly my destiny is changed completely. Since I have you, bad luck is mine no longer. It can never be mine again. If I face death and die tonight my last breath will still know joy.

LINDA. Tonight is enough. For a moment I wished tonight could be forever. But some grand new feeling tells me our destiny has further to go.

SIEGMUND. I had planned to kill Hunding, and take you with me, although I was just a lone outlaw. But now I can see a much greater future for you.

LINDA. Whether Hunding lives or dies we've got to be away before morning.

SIEGMUND. Yes, but he must live. The whole establishment must not start questioning all the guests who've been coming here. I've been planning our strategy. You leave a note that says nothing of our meeting and departure other than our personal love.

LINDA. Oh, that's enough, its more than enough. But I know your meaning. I know what I'll say. We are very much alike in appearance; I will say you are my brother. Hunding knows I was only two years old when my parents were killed and he could believe it. I will say you learned the story, have trailed my kidnapers for years, and have taken me back with you to the wilds.

SIEGMUND. That's perfect. You *are* my comrade in arms. You're my dream of love but you are also a warrior. As a warrior, you will tell me where and with whom to make contacts in the capital, and I will raise a force in the wilds to march and join them. We will not be defeated. Our love will add strength to my arm and wisdom to my strategy. This great deed, that has waited so long for its doing, is going to find in me a worthy leader. Both love and destiny are making me their willing instrument. Already in my mind I see my men forming in the woods and mountains. They are all good men. They can always be trusted.

LINDA. What about the men here? *(She has been writing the note at the table.)*

SIEGMUND. They are more difficult to picture. But I can almost see them too. They will separate from the dross that has grown around them like a sharp sword from its mouldy scabbard. *(He straightens his dishevelled clothes, tightens his belt, picks up a coat and places it around Linda.)* This victory I will give you as a bride gift. It will bring you your freedom and bring freedom to all who would become love's champions. So now you must come with me, leave this house of love's enemy, come out from the city, and we will go to the only home I know, out into the wildsland. It's spring there now and the whole forest is waiting in full glory to welcome you back where you belong. *(He puts his arm around her shoulder and takes her with him.)*

Curtain.

23

ACT TWO

Outside a luxurious residence in Valhalla, the golden-orange sunlight of early morning falls on a large brick terrace. There is a wide expanse of beautiful park-like grounds.

Wotan sits in a comfortable lounge chair on the terrace with his morning coffee. From around the building comes his daughter, Brunnhilde. She is a handsomely beautiful girl in a very short, very dashing, parade-like uniform with an ornamented sword. She is singing, shouting, half-dancing, half-executing a proud military march. Before Wotan, she comes to a smart military halt, draws her sword, presents arms, thrusts her sword back, bends over and kisses him, stands back at attention again — all done just from the joy of movement that comes from exuberant youth. Finally she executes "at ease" with military precision and waits for Wotan to speak.

WOTAN. Have your planes polished to glittering brightness. Have your corps of Valkyries dressed in their finest uniforms. A great fight has broken out in Nibelung. Siegmund leads many valiant warriors. There was a major battle yesterday, continuing through the night. Many are wounded. Rumor has it that among them is Siegmund himself. Your Valkyries must fly to Nibelung to remove the wounded, and thereby give Siegmund some encouragement.

BRUNNHILDE. *(snaps to attention, salutes, bends and kisses him again, starts across the grounds, then turns back to tell him.)* I warn you, father. Steel yourself. There's a major battle in store for you right here. Your devoted wife, Fricka, in her most wifely attitude, is on her way. She knows the battle in Nibelung started yesterday. She's firmly set against your endorsement of Siegmund's forces. She plans to have it out with you. Battle in the field I love, with clean issues and strong men. Both the issues and the weapons here seem sticky and coated with rust. So I'm running away. Father, you are left in the lurch. *(She disappears around the building.)*

FRICKA. *(approaches from the other side, anger in her manner of walk. She begins talking before she reaches Wotan.)* You breakfasted early and disappeared. You were trying to avoid me, I know. I called the office and the hall but you hadn't been seen. So to save you from your folly, I've had to track you down.

WOTAN. I wish you were more woman and less manipulator; but, since you're here, we'll go over it again.

FRICKA. The issue is as clear as day. You know that I have publicly identified myself with the sanctity of marriage. Along with that goes the right of a husband to protect the honor of his wife and daughters. Half the people believe this fight between Siegmund and Hunding is purely personal. Under these conditions I say that you must *not* endorse Siegmund's action.

WOTAN. *(patiently)* Even if the fight were personal, I would not be convinced to withhold my endorsement. The moral issues are stronger than the convention of marriage. Love ruled before men learned to babble words about "who gives this woman." None will find me the enemy of love's might.

FRICKA. You are trying to appear very obtuse. You know that without the formality of marriage all society crumbles. And you know that if a man must assume obligations by the ceremony, he must also be granted rights.

WOTAN. Yet this much is basic: unholy is the bond that binds unloving hearts. A convention that supports such a bond needs to be reexamined. I came to power while advocating mortal combat among strong men — when their differences were irreconcilable. Should I then reverse my commitment to individual sovereignty? Should I advocate binding a woman, whose virtue is not strength but tenderness, by conditions where her freedom of choice must be suppressed, must be allowed to fester and destroy the tenderness of her heart?

FRICKA. *(stops moving about to confront him more directly.)* If marriage as we know it is to be called unholy, with what would you replace it? Free love you know cannot be sanctioned. Not even the most primitive society can develop under its influence. And wherever it shows up in mature civilizations, it can be recognized, either as a contributing cause, or as a symptom of their decadence. I have never heard you question marriage as an institution before.

WOTAN. Well, you hear me now. And I have often questioned it in my thoughts. There is a great flaw. The convention considers the man more than the woman. The relationship is one of love, and any marriage convention should hold love sacred to a sovereign woman, just as the right to do battle is sacred to a man. Material possessions always seem to create the problem. The problem is not intrinsic within them, but because they are involved, marriage, which should listen only to love, must heed also the voice of legality.

FRICKA. Flaws can be found in all conventions by someone whose interest it is to find them. And marriage is no exception. But since by treaty we have no actual control in world affairs, the sovereigns, looked upon as gods, must make the most of our prestige by selecting where to give our nods of approval. I, wife of the gods' chief, have pointed up that licentiousness and free love in FAFNER and FASOLT were evidence of their decadence. I have said that they were a contributing factor to their downfall. I have made much of the continuing evils of physical and statutory rape. And I have said that the defence against them is the sanctity of the home and the sacredness of the marraige vows. Your endorsement of Siegmund's cause, when all know that Siegmund and Linda have been living together for months out of wedlock, would be a blow to the prestige of the gods. And particularly would my prestige be hurt.

WOTAN. Your prestige plays too big a role in your thoughts.

FRICKA. It cannot suffer much more. Every time I talk of marriage, all are reminded of your own unfaithfulness. Year after year you returned to Nibelung as a private individual to study conditions, but while there you lived with Erda and "embraced her soul" — "a true being, whose body and soul were one." Then you brought back here to Godsland the fruit of the fickle fancy, a bold and defiant maiden, another "daughter of the earth." You created for her a position of high influence as Chief of the Valkyries.

WOTAN. Brunnhilde does more to uphold our prestige than all the rest of us put together.

FRICKA. (ignores the interruption.) The Swan Maidens, caring for and removing the wounded, honoring the dead and bringing them here for burial, and thereby giving hope to their families that they still lived — that was good and useful. And it was fitting that beautiful young girls be used for the purpose. But when the daughter of Erda was placed in charge, the corps' name became Valkyrie, their demure uniforms were exchanged for those of dashing girl warriors, and they dropped from the skies in their polished planes before battle, to comfort and assure the men they would be *ready* to remove the wounded — and to inspire heroism, and rashness, and wounds, and death, until it is said that to see the face of a Valkyrie is to die. Such price to men's lives is what you pay to raise theValkyries to prestige, but your wife you would allow to be trampled over in scorn.

WOTAN. (remains quiet as he answers her.) You cannot learn because you will not that I have made no concession to the Valkyries. Brunnhilde knows my heart and my wish before I know it myself. Her change in the corps was her idea but it was my own wish unknown to myself. I grieve for futile bravery and bloodshed when there is no chance, but death before fetters — even those of gold, padded with silk, and studded with jewels — I have learned too late should be chosen before the first small verbal compromise. Brunnhilde does not inspire rashness. She inspires steadfastness and honor. And these we must have. Strategy is a thing of battle, but compromise must not be given that name.

FRICKA. Your present strategy seems to be getting away from the subject. We were talking about your wish to endorse Siegmund.

WOTAN. I have made treaties that make me regret the day I was born. I have bound myself by words and I cannot remove my own bonds. It is a frequent price man must pay for his language. But if man is to be more than other animals, honor must be more than life. I have an enemy that I know can be conquered only with a sword, but mine cannot be the hand that holds it, nor my voice give the command that directs its holder. What I can do is very little, but I would see the prestige of the gods reduced to a cavity in the earth rather than see it deflect by so much as a breeze's faint whisper that sword point from its true target. I think Siegmund might do for the gods what we cannot do for ourselves.

FRICKA. Our position has become one of upholding ideals. What can a young upstart contribute to the stature of those ideals when only by conformity does he gain endorsement?

WOTAN. We try but to recognize man's being at its best; the being itself we cannot modify. We should not try. Our ideals should try to mark a path we have found worth traveling, not program men as the police-states program zombis.

FRICKA. By the gods' endorsement men should be encouraged to hold to ideals of proven worth. But by the gods' endorsement you try to spur men to resist the established order of things in Nibelung.

WOTAN. *(begins to show the emotion of the heavy thoughts that come to his mind but tries to carry on in an even tone.)* Siegmund grew unaided. His ideals he has chosen for himself. He fights in my name, and by treaty I cannot help him. But by treaty I can remove the wounded. And I will.

FRICKA. *(notes his emotion and begins to bear down.)* The gods have the only planes left in the world. When they come from the sky to comfort one side, the effect is tremendous. The rumored uprising in the capital may hang on their appearance.

WOTAN. *(sits up straight with seeming surprise.)* What uprising in the capital?

FRICKA. Don't lie by feigning surprise. You know that is what you hope for. You have dreamed of nothing else since you first fanned hope to flame and promised your followers in Nibelung a leader.

WOTAN. *(his voice increasingly unsteady)* I have followed the treaty to the letter. If there's an uprising Siegmund inspired it.

FRICKA. *(without letup of pressure)* You know that Siegmund's will to fight, passed down through his father before him, was inspired by you, as was also whatever will to fight still remains among the people of the capital. I know the rule has been oppressive and the will-to-vengeance needs no inspiration, but you planned to regain Nibelung even while conceding it, planned to have it come voluntarily under your rule. That I approved; the treaty was clear. And you have adhered to its terms — until now. *(She notes that the thrust went home and continues confidently.)* Brunnhilde knows the stakes of this fight, and has said she will make a speech to the warriors that will inspire them to battle as never before. She knows their weakness is their inability to out-maneuver Hunding's fast cavalry. She has said she will even act as spotter from the air and keep Siegmund informed. *(Wotan starts to make another protesting gesture, then seems to fall before Fricka's continuing accusation.)* You weaken first on the sanctity of marriage, where there might be room for doubt, but when one ideal begins to waver, others follow close behind, until all the gods represent is in question, and you would wink at actual violation of treaty.

WOTAN. *(gloomily)* What is truly right here?

FRICKA. *(without hesitation)* Order the Valkyries not to fly.

WOTAN. They can at least remove the wounded.

FRICKA. If you will not protect my honor, protect your own. See that they give no aid.

WOTAN. I have neither ordered nor consented to aid.

FRICKA. You cannot fool me and don't fool yourself. You know Brunnhilde's intention.

WOTAN. The Valkyries have their orders.

FRICKA. True. But you said, yourself, Brunnhilde acts only to accomplish your will. She knows the orders you would give her if you could.

WOTAN. One word to Siegmund of Hunding's movements could mean the difference between success or failure.

FRICKA. You must order Brunnhilde not to speak that word — even if it means he does not reach the capital, or his allies in the capital show themselves and are destroyed.

(Brunnhilde is heard calling across the grounds.)

You can hear your valorous daughter now — shouting as if it were *her* battle.

WOTAN. I have already given orders that the Valkyries will fly.

FRICKA. Then let them guard as they can the honor of the gods. You're wrong, I feel, completely wrong, not to stand clearly for the sanctity of marriage. But on the treaty, you, even you, know there can be no slightest breach of terms. Make this clear to Brunnhilde. Promise me that.

WOTAN. *(speaks half to himself in terrible dejection.)* Have I gone so far that honor must be an oath?

FRICKA. *(strides away and speaks to Brunnhilde in passing.)* Your father is waiting to give you instructions.

BRUNNHILDE. *(anxiously approaches Wotan as he sits brooding in deep gloom.)* I'm afraid the fight did not end well. Fricka is angry at the outcome, and you are despondent. Are there any changes in instructions? *(She notices fully the change that has come over Wotan and asks in a more sympathetic tone.)* What troubles you, father? What makes you so downcast? You know you can tell me?

WOTAN. *(sadly)* I am bound by self-forged fetters and am least free of all things living.

BRUNNHILDE. Father, I don't understand you like this. Can't you tell me what awful thing gnaws at your heart?

WOTAN. *(moves his head and shoulders about as if to test the position of physical bonds.)* Fettered freedom! Blasphemed sanctity! Grievous joy! Every issue has become tied to another that is unrelated. I am most sorrowful of all creatures still living.

BRUNNHILDE. *(alarmed, unbuckles her sword, lays it aside, and kneels with anxious affection at his knees.)* Father! Father! What deep thing disturbs you? Confide in me for I am true. I beg you. *(She lays her hand and head with tender anxiety on his knees and breast.)*

WOTAN. *(looks long into her eyes then strokes her head with involuntary tenderness. As if coming out of a deep reverie, he at last says, very slowly.)* What if, when uttered, my words made weaker the controlling might of my will?

BRUNNHILDE. *(very softly)* To Wotan's will you speak when you speak to me. What am I if I am not your will?

WOTAN. *(responding to her tone)* What never was to any spoken shall be unspoken now and forever; myself I speak to when speaking to you. *(He pauses to collect his thoughts.)* We try to uphold our sovereign ideals and our way of life as shining and flawless — not through vanity that hides behind lies — but with sincere purpose. As a child must have food while still unable to distinguish figs from thistles, so must men and women act before they have had time to evaluate ideals still in formation. Otherwise they become sad monks in monasteries, nuns reaching blindly for goodness, or philosophers growing old in childhood with the burden of study and analysis. *(Brunnhilde sits up, looks at him, and follows his words attentively.)* All beauty must be born of joy and truth, and joy is the fruit of living in the moment. That much most men recognize; their innate wisdom grasps a brief workable code of conduct, and they pick some simple goal, so they can begin to live. But simple codes of conduct are seldom complete or perfect. Marriage as an institution, Fricka would have me uphold as so. That I will not do, even though I have not opposed her words committing herself to its sanctity. A woman's right to choose her lover without coercion and without restraint, is something nearer to my liking.

BRUNNHILDE. Fricka says she opposes rape and whoredom.

WOTAN. Rape and whoredom, of course, none will countenance. But a relation as disgusting as either is often condoned if it has been masked by a marriage ceremony. And often the horror it hides outweighs whatever good a marriage ceremony may support. For his relation to Linda, I would not for a moment withhold aid from Siegmund.

BRUNNHILDE. *(showing a momentary joy)* Then, in your fight with Fricka, you did not both lose. I shall fly as planned. You have made no compromise.

WOTAN. Oh, that your words were true, and I had made no compromise. Then you would fly with joy — as would Donner — and we would know full victory. But I have compromised — not now with Fricka — I did not agree to further muddy our sovereign ideals. I will never add to them another ideal alloyed with poisonous establishment practices. The trouble is that they already have been tainted beyond my power to purify.

BRUNNHILDE. What of Siegmund's ideals, father?

WOTAN. Siegmund's ideals are yet simple and pure. He fights for individual freedom and dignity — and for love. On these I would stake our sovereign prestige without equivocation. ... My sadness is that I yearn to aid him and cannot. I would aid him both because I believe in his purpose and because his victory might be the salvation of all sovereigns. He might open public opinion to our reception.

BRUNNHILDE. Public opinion? Father, that does not sound like you.

WOTAN. *(in an explanatory tone)* The power that I want is not physical. It is the opportunity to appeal to people's minds and the chance to purify the ideals I have helped to contaminate. Erda — your mother — says it would do no good, that it would lead only to destruction. She is wise and her warning weighs heavily on me, but I would like to try. It is my only hope. I cannot turn back from the course to which I'm committed.

BRUNNHILDE. What could you do in this way?

WOTAN. Listen carefully and I will try to tell you. ... The lure that leads men in daily life is not always an ideal so big that they will fight and die for it. The rulers of the police-state, and all who seek power merely for the sake of power, try to confuse and muddy all ideals. The method is to identify each ideal with an irrelevant issue. When the confusion is great enough, no one will take any big action. Then the lure that leads people in their daily life can be moved in any direction in such small steps that strong opposition appears ridiculous.

BRUNNHILDE. Yes, father. I have not known that but I see that it could happen.

WOTAN. That is the method that the police-states' rulers use to brainwash their zombis. At one time the lure became simply faddishness in entertainment. A Ring was awarded for the television program that attracted the most viewers. The Ring became a handy symbol for whatever lure is attracting the most people on a worldwide scale.

BRUNNHILDE. Yes, I am following you.

WOTAN. Whenever manufactured articles are used merely as emblems of prestige, they can be fashioned into a Ring. This was once very widely done, and this was done by Alber in the part of the wilds that was my field of action. Because I, myself, chose a simple life, and because I warned others against what he was doing, his propaganda identified me, and all who wanted individual sovereignty, with the lazy and incompetent, with those who sought but could not succeed in getting the coveted manufactured possessions. I made the mistake of trying to beat him at the Ring game; I bargained for Valhalla. But the bargain led to compromise, compromise to dishonest acts, and finally to the treaty of which you are well aware.

BRUNNHILDE. Yes, I know. Your own treaty has bound you to inaction.

WOTAN. Now I can take no hand in the areas where the major battles for men's lives and ideals are being fought. We sovereigns can only enter to observe conditions or remove the wounded. It keeps our memory and ideal alive in the hearts of some men, and sometimes gives them courage to fight — a fight I know to be good but cannot aid. I cannot melt up the alloy of confused ideals and distil one pure unless I can gain control of the Ring which Alber fashioned and the rulers of FAFNER now hold. One only can take it for all sovereigns by a deed of valor — one not protected or aided by me.

BRUNNHILDE. Siegmund could do it. I didn't know all that about the Ring but I knew you wanted Siegmund's victory, and that you were treaty bound not to help him. That seems the basic problem. Is that right?

WOTAN. *(nods agreement.)* I condemn the dwarfs for letting themselves be made into slaves, yet I have done the same as they. I, who am called the chief god of freedom and beauty, am bound by fetters I myself have fashioned. I am worse than the dwarfs because those I would aid would, by that aid, be made slaves to my treaties.

BRUNNHILDE. *(tries to reason through the obstacle.)* Siegmund speaks to his men of your ideals but he fights his own battle.

WOTAN. It is a battle the taste for which I have done everything I could to sharpen. Before the treaty my acts to this end I consider honorable. I deliberately planted seeds of revolt in Nibelung even while I planned to deliver it to the established nations. But that was not dishonorable. It was done openly. I had never agreed to anything more than delivery of control. However since that time I have had to watch myself closely.

BRUNNHILDE. Everyone knows you have always adhered to the treaty.

WOTAN. I have emphasized the proud beauty of the Valkyries and the dormant power of Donner's forces, while removing wounded as permitted by treaty. In so doing I have strained honesty close to the breaking point. In this important battle I might have brought wide public dishonor on all sovereigns and their ideals by permitting honor to overstrain and break. But Fricka saw the danger and showed me that to which my desire for Siegmund's victory might have made me blind.

BRUNNHILDE. *(increduously)* Would you do now what would deprive Siegmund of victory?

WOTAN. I have compromised with the enemy I fight, and in compromise always hides a curse. I have to guard my frustrated passion constantly. I must even examine my motives to insure that, in self-deceit, I am not bringing wounded warriors to Valhalla lest the sadness and decadence of sovereigns gathered here should cry out for new blood, as did the cities of the police-states when they were led to prey upon the free. Should that day dawn, I must find strength to destroy all sovereigns with my own hands, before they become a sterile monument to curse-poisoned pomp. *(He rises in bitter wrath that tenses his whole body.)* Oh, that I were free to hand back to those who covet it the glitter and poisoned pomp of the "Men Like Gods", and watch them consume it with their envious greed.

BRUNNHILDE. *(alarmed by his behavior)* Father, tell me. What task do you give your child?

WOTAN. *(bitterly)* You will go to Siegmund and give such encouragement as your mere presence affords. But you will bring back the wounded and nothing more. You shall give no advice on strategy. And you shall *not* observe and inform Siegmund of Hunding's movements.

BRUNNHILDE. Oh, father, take back those instructions. You

love Siegmund as if he were your own son, and your hopes have been high for this victory. Let me aid — only with words — at my own discretion.

WOTAN. *(firmly)* You shall give no aid by word or act. The odds are strongly against Siegmund and fast information of Hunding's movements, such as only an air observer could give, would help to give Siegmund an equal chance. But you shall not give that information. That is clear. And it is not a request from father to daughter; it is an *order* from her commander to the Valkyrie Chief.

BRUNNHILDE. *(straightening herself up)* Your reasoning is too complex for me to fully understand, but two things are clear. One, you are not positive that the ideals you uphold are without flaw. Two, you are so certain of your endorsement of Siegmund that you cause serious hurt to Fricka to make it effective. So despite your warning, I will give Siegmund such aid as I can.

WOTAN. *(explosively)* No! Don't you dare defy my clear order! As a Valkyrie, what are you? You are nothing but a symbol I have created and as such you are the choiceless, blind slave of my will! Have I sunk so low by showing my mind that my own daughter, hardly more than a child, holds me in scorn. Do you, child, know my wrath? If ever its awful lightning struck you then you would know a hell such as you have never dreamed. Within my being burns enough rage to lay waste in dread ruins a world that I yearn to see wearing nothing but smiles. So understand this: Don't call forth my rage; carry out my commands. Give Siegmund no aid! You know the clear limits of the Valkyries task. Stick to them! *(He storms away and disappears around the corner of the house.)*

BRUNNHILDE. *(watches Wotan go then takes a long breath as if the air had been too thick to breathe.)* I have often seen my warfather enraged but never once like this. *(She stoops sadly down, takes up her sword and buckles it on.)* How heavy my heart feels now! To inspire warriors has been glorious but now I could only bring discouragement. *(She gazes into space visualizing her task.)* Woe to you Siegmund. With great sorrow must I, who could have given you victory, falsely forsake you! *(She turns and walks dejectedly across the grounds while the light seems to fade from the world.)*

* * *

(Darkness becomes total and, in the darkness, time and place cease to exist for a moment while the focus of the most critical of world events moves to a spot a slight distance from a crude, hastily set up military headquarters hidden in the woods. Siegmund and Linda are alone at the foot of a tree. Siegmund has wounds on head, shoulder and leg. Linda, herself totally exhausted, tries to make him more comfortable. He tries to keep her quietly beside him.)

34

SIEGMUND. You must rest now. You can't help by killing yourself.

LINDA. Have we a chance?

SIEGMUND. That surprise by Hunding was a big setback.

LINDA. *(wearily)* Have we a chance?

SIEGMUND. How different things look now from that night when we fled across the hills in the moonlight. Then we were filled more with our own love than with the fate of men who would stand ready to die with us. Remember how happy we were then? We were full of hope. We were entirely carefree. We ran, leaping — almost flying — over little streams as if we were as weightless as the clouds in the moonlit sky above us. *(Linda shows new weariness and he pulls her down beside him.)* You must rest; we march soon after sunset. There are clouds and the darkness will come early. You must have strength, for you move up with us; you are my comrade still, as well as my bride.

LINDA. I'm your evil spirit. I've brought you only misfortune. If there had been less haste, and this push planned for next year, its chance of success would have been greater. *(He starts to protest but she puts her finger over his mouth.)* The madness of my dreams affected your cool reason. My love is pure but my body is shamed and dishonored; it could not forget the memory of horrid nights, nights when it writhed with hate and loathing. The memory tormented my dreams, woke me screaming in terror, and built in you an uncontrollable hate of Hunding. That hate affected what should have been cooler planning. ...I should have killed myself early, before marriage to that foul creature. That I was a child was my only excuse. But I was not a child when you met me. It was evil to give you a corpse, a corpse that should have been purified by burning, and had its ashes scattered to the winds. But in your embrace I have loved you truly, with a rapture pure and a bliss of the sweetest. My sense and soul were steeped in delight, and knew joy and beauty unblemished. Only in my dreams was that house remembered, and only screams in my sleeping told you of that horror. But the haste brought on by that telling may have been the undoing of plans that were truly noble.

SIEGMUND. The plans are not undone, and defeat has not been acknowledged. We have suffered a severe blow but Hunding will not try to stop us from moving up in the darkness. If the forces in the capital come forth when they see our attack, the battle could yet be won. If not, at least we die fighting.

LINDA. Listen, I heard a bugle. Hunding may attack *before* darkness. There may be no chance to fight in the city streets where allies will rally to the battle. *(She pauses a long moment to get strength to talk further.)* Darling, let's speak plainly, for we are one and this much I know: Even if victory should come it will not be yours and mine. I know you are brave even to highest folly, and I would not have you otherwise, but your wounds are deep; that you still live is a miracle. I know you could not travel an hour without paying the last price. And yet you will try to lead and fight tomorrow, so that your death in battle may be not less than those whom you lead to their final defeat. That I am here when I might hide in a village has caused you little concern, and with good reason. You know you face certain defeat and you know Hunding has sworn to destroy everyone connected with the uprising. You know he will find me if it takes his lifetime. *(She throws herself sobbing on his chest, then sits up and continues.)* For you I grieve, that I have brought you this defeat. But for myself I cannot stop, even by shaming it as selfish, the joy that is mine to have known and loved you, and to have the bliss of dying at your side. Never before I saw the courage and hope in your eyes had I dreamed of more than death with honor. Now that will be mine, made rich by our months of joy.

SIEGMUND. *(knowing he can give her no answer in words, only holds her closer and speaks softly.)* My comrade. My beloved.

(He holds her in his arms, listens to her breathing and, as she sleeps from weariness, eases her down while he remains propped against the tree with her head resting on his knee. He watches over her with tender concern; meanwhile his own wounds take their toll until sounds, lights and shadows make disjointed impressions that convey no consistent picture of reality.)

(While he is in this state, Brunnhilde finds him. Twilight has deepened but a last light through the trees falls upon her. She pauses and watches from a distance, then advances slowly again and stops when she gets nearer. She stands motionless, with erect military bearing.)

BRUNNHILDE. Siegmund! A hero, but a wounded leader of many wounded men.

SIEGMUND. *(looking up, cannot believe what his eyes tell him, but whether in life, dreams, or death, he has the same directness of approach.)* Who are you, tell me, that you come and stand so fair and stern?

BRUNNHILDE. I am a Valkyrie of the gods. *(She studies him carefully before she continues.)* I would have spoken to your men before battle. I see it is too late. I can only remove wounded heroes who shall live and will again fight.

SIEGMUND. Do I dream? *(He asks the question both of her and of himself.)* Or can the Valkyries be real and not merely legend?

BRUNNHILDE. You do not dream. *(Although her words sound real, her military bearing remains as unmoving as if she were a vision.)* Your lieutenant says you are unable to fight further. I, myself, will fly you to Valhalla.

SIEGMUND. Why should I go to Valhalla? My place is here.

BRUNNHILDE. You can but die by staying. There you can recover, meet many great heroes, and prepare for the battles Wotan can fight.

SIEGMUND. Wotan does not fight here; and in Godsland, according to legend, his power is unquestioned. What need has he for warriors?

BRUNNHILDE. There are some wildslands where he may still do battle. Here treaty prohibits it.

SIEGMUND. Could I return here myself and fight?

BRUNNHILDE. Not after accepting the protection of the gods.

SIEGMUND. Then I will not go. What place has Valhalla for women?

BRUNNHILDE. The gods are noted for their beauty. You would find Valhalla's halls happy with women's laughter.

SIEGMUND. It is not for myself that I ask about women but for Linda. Could she have such a place as yours?

BRUNNHILDE. It would not be impossible but she would have to come of herself and the way is long and difficult. I could not take her. Treaty permits me to remove only heroes wounded in battle.

SIEGMUND. I shall be grateful for those you aid and those who would go with you, go with my blessing. But you waste time talking to me: I will not go.

BRUNNHILDE. *(moves forward a pace but retains her military bearing. Her voice is slightly less formal as she continues.)* Your men say your wounds are deep and the handicap of their leader is more discouraging than the many dead and wounded. They have great faith in your leadership and your judgment. Your refusal to go with me under the circumstances I understand and respect. *(She pauses thoughtfully.)* Are there any chances for success in tomorrow's battle — despite the heavy losses?

SIEGMUND. *(listens for Linda's breathing to insure that she is asleep.)* There will be no battle tomorrow. When darkness comes I will give orders not to move up but to disperse. That's our only defense. We have lost our main objective for my lifetime.

BRUNNHILDE. I know courage is not lacking. Were your losses today so heavy?

SIEGMUND. Our losses were heavy but my men are brave and our strategy is good and well planned. If we could gain the city we might yet win. We have allies there who would identify themselves, give shelter and aid. Spread out through the city, we could defeat Hunding in small groups and single combat. His men are cowards; they always lose their will to fight when not massed.

BRUNNHILDE. The plan is good and you still have men. Why do you abandon hope of getting to the city?

SIEGMUND. We are greatly out numbered; surprise was necessary. There are two points of attack. We thought Hunding would expect the west side. We planned to feint there with a small force, draw his big force, then enter the city from the east. He guessed our strategy. We tried to make him think he had guessed wrong, retreated with a show of weakness, drew him farther and farther into the woods, and hurt him more than he hurt us. But I'm convinced we did not fool him, we did not make him believe this was the diversionary force. He knows now where we are and how few we are. Only if he thought this was really a diversion, and that a greater force was in the west, would he use his forces as we planned, and we would have a chance. I'm convinced he will not think so, and on the chance I will not waste my men and induce a show of allies in the city.

BRUNNHILDE. *(Her voice becomes a little louder and carries a probing touch of scorn.)* So your men disperse, and your allies in the city wait another generation for a leader that may not come. And what happens to you?

SIEGMUND. Quiet. Don't wake Linda. The men disperse and continue to fight where and when they can. Some day another chance may come, though I hope not at the price that was paid for this one. Linda here alone made it possible by the fate she suffered in becoming acquainted and arousing sympathy and faith in the city. For my life I care nothing except as it has become precious to her. For her this victory was to be. But the bravest, saddest, and most ill-starred of women is to have not even that good for her suffering. She must face death in the arms of a beaten warrior and a leader who has had nothing but ignominious defeat.

BRUNNHILDE. Your only thought is love of wife and comrades. Your own life you give without hesitation. You only grieve that it is small and will not hold back the tide you would dam with it.

SIEGMUND. You, who stand before me so young and fair that I doubted not your bravery and sweetness to be such as Linda's, though untouched by her sorrow — do you show surprise that I love and my love is of my whole being? You, who are the gods, do you not love even so? Have our dreams and ideals been given to us by those who are less then we?

BRUNNHILDE. That question too has disturbed me as I think it distrubed my mother. Let me hide Linda with some distant family and take you to Valhalla where your great soul may add stature to the gods.

SIEGMUND. My wife shall never again wake to find another than I guarding her. When Hunding's horsemen come, as they must, mine will be the hand that slays her.

BRUNNHILDE. *(Her emotion shows by the loss of her military bearing.)* Siegmund! Madman! Listen to me. Entrust her to me for the sake of the pledge which she carries of you and your love.

SIEGMUND. Only for hope of victory would I have sent her away to safety before tomorrow's battle. Since it is not to be fought *(he draws his sword)* before she awakes this sword shall take both hers and the life that beats within her.

BRUNNHILDE. *(moves forward, bends down, and reaches out her arms almost as if she would take the sword from him.)* No, Siegmund, no! Listen to me! Spare Linda, entrust her to me; and move forward tonight toward the city and tomorrow's victory. A god, too, can sacrifice a lover, who with bravery and love would make the sacrifice gladly. Hunding shall expect a heavy attack from the west and will move all his forces there, leaving you a clear field to enter from your present position. *(Bugles are heard in the distance.)* He is sounding retreat now to prepare for tomorrow's battle. You, too, prepare, and trust to your allies in the city. And trust me; I will help you. I will fly over Hunding's forces conspicuously. That will arouse speculation and alarm as to my purpose. But more than that I will do. I know Hunding checks all Valkyries reports on the radio. Tomorrow, before dawn, in time to draw off his forces, he will hear a report such as he has half feared and half hoped for since I took command. I will say that I am giving you full support. He might think my purpose is what it is. To be sure I do not fail you, I will address myself to a certain lieutenant of the gods' warriors and ask him to join me in the battle for the glory of the gods. I know what reply Hunding will hear: A strong, confident voice from Valhalla giving that long unheard battle cry of a god who stakes all. It cannot fail to convince Hunding. Leave Linda here until after the battle, but have your men help you move forward tonight; they will need your courage and direction for this daring. *(She rushes away and disappears, leaving Siegmund gazing after her, joyful and exultant.)*

SIEGMUND. *(bends over Linda and listens to her breathing.)* How soundly sleeps my poor darling in her heavy exhaustion. Almost it seems she knows, even in her sleep, the change in fate that is ours. She smiles as if remembering happiness, and seldom have I seen her sleep untroubled. I'll not waken her now but return and tell her the good news after speaking with my other comrades.

(He lays her gently on the embankment and kisses her brow, then rises unsteadily.) My joy has lent healing to my own wounds. I feel like a man reborn. I can stand and address my men, giving them courage by my strength, and lending confidence and proud bearing to my good words. *(He draws his sword to prepare for his entrance before his men and practices that entrance by raising it aloft and rehearsing the words to greet them.)* My sword thirsts for Hunding's blood. *(He goes with unsteady but strengthening steps toward his men.)*

(Sudden blackness envelops everything as time and space dissolve. There is thunder and lightening and the sounds of battle. The critical developments in the affairs of men become divided into two focal points — shown as insets on separate sides of stage — with communication between them by radio; the principals are Hunding and Wotan.

(Hunding hovers over a technician who is manipulating a radio. The technician hands a microphone to Hunding who grabs it and speaks into it angrily.)

HUNDING. Wotan, what does this mean? I have heard messages that sound like breach of treaty from the Valkyrie to your headquarters and an answering cry from your own headquarters that, legend has it, no god can utter and continue to live without victory. My troops have rushed to the rendezvous point, and found only the Valkryie's lone plane dipping at my troops, trying to disrupt the cavalry.

(Wotan and his warrior guards are assembled around another radio in Valhalla and another technician hands a microphone to Wotan.)

WOTAN. I have been trying to get the Valkyrie since the message came in but she does not answer. Ignore her. She does not — I repeat, does *not* — speak for the gods. One lone lieutenant tried to go to her aid and was shot down by my orders. She has no force and nothing she does affects your plans. I am leaving now to deal with the rebel.

HUNDING. Siegmund is moving into the city from the east and the plan is now apparent. I can yet stop him and break the traitor band in my own capital. But the Valkyrie has broken treaty and I will demand reparations.

WOTAN. Though I would give my soul to see you in hell, I will stand by my treaty. You shall have full legal reparations.

(Hunding fades from the focus of world affairs but the scene surrounding Wotan remains. He hands the microphone back to the technician, stands a moment in tense immobility, then the welling anger within breaks into violent rage.)

40

WOTAN. Brunnhilde! Brunnhilde! The emotional, headstrong, guilty rebel. The heavens help her! Ready my plane for flight to Nibelung. She shall not again touch Valhalla!

Curtain.

ACT THREE

On a mountain top before the ruins of a deserted castle, there are broken columns and broken pieces of statuary. Vines and trees, grown up amidst the ruins, show the castle's long abandonment. Lower down, out of sight, there is an abandoned landing field. Four Valkyries who have just landed are moving about or standing on pieces of broken columns for a better view of additional planes that are coming in. All wear the Valkyries' dashing uniforms with swords.

FIRST V. *(calling out cheerfully and waving with her sword to someone unseen down in the landing field)* Good landing! That was a tight squeeze. ... That brush keeps growing and the landing field is smaller every year.

(The other Valkyries also wave; cheerful voices offstage answer.)

SECOND V. *(calling to those on landing field—in a more serious tone)* Siegmund was already dead and the fight at the edge of the capital was dying before we left. What's happened since?

THIRD V. *(adds her own anxious question).* Was there an uprising in the city?

FIFTH V. *(comes into view as she answers)* There was some guerrilla action; the fight's now moving to the woods.

FOURTH V. Siegmund's men are real heroes. They fight as long as they breathe, but with such a battle we soon had our planes loaded to capacity.

FIRST V. I have an overload. But one more handsome hero I had to take.

SECOND V. *(springs up, starts toward the field, but comes back.)* I thought my nurse was signalling — but she was just shouting in play.

(Several Valkyries laugh with understanding.)

FIRST V. Those nurses are going to have their hands full with these men. Their bodies recover the minute they become conscious.

SECOND V. *(calls down to her nurse with laughter.)* If they're recovering that fast, I'll give you some help. *(Some signal reassures her that all is well; she signals back, then focuses with the others on a new arrival.)*

THIRD V. *(calling out to the new arrival)* What took you so long?

43

SIXTH V. *(coming on stage)* I had to go back twice and let a newly conscious man out. These men don't know when they're knocked out of battle.

(There is more noise and shouted greetings from those in the field.)

SECOND V. Did you see those planes come in?

THIRD V. Yeah, they landed side by side.

FOURTH V. *(calling a comment on the daring landing as two more Valkyries come on stage)* Greeting, valiant Valkyries. *(All welcome the newcomers.)*

SEVENTH and EIGHTH V. Hi, you there.

SECOND V. After that exhibition I suppose you'll want us all to take off between these trees in formation.

FIFTH V. We're going to have to clear that brush or find a new rendezvous field.

FOURTH V. Any change in battle in the last hour?

EIGHTH V. No. It's settling into retreat and guerrilla action. Could last months.

SEVENTH V. If we're assembled, why aren't we taking off for Valhalla. I feel lost now that all radios have been scrapped to keep Brunnhilde's in repair.

FIFTH V. Brunnhilde's not here yet; she may have received some new orders.

FIRST V. Something seemed strange. I saw her flying over Hunding's forces almost at ground level.

THIRD V. I'm sure nothing could have gone wrong, but I saw her take off from the battle in an odd direction. We should wait for her here and return together as usual.

SIXTH V. There she is! She came in low and her plane was wobbling. A wing looks damaged.

ALL V. *(wave and shout.)* Brunnhilde, hi. *(There is no answer.)*

VARIOUS V. That plane is either damaged or overloaded. ...That was a rough landing. ...Her plane has no room for much overload. ...She has no nurse and only room for one stretcher.

SECOND V. *(with great surprise)* Her hero isn't much wounded; he's getting out with her!

FIFTH V. That's a woman, see!

FIRST V. I wonder what this means.

FOURTH V. Has she no greeting for her Valkyries.

THIRD V. *(loudly)* Heiaha! Brunnhilde! *(There is no answer.)* Heiaha! Brunnhilde! Can you hear me? *(Still no answer.)*

SECOND V. *(starting toward the field)* Let's go see if she needs any help.

THIRD V. She's having trouble getting the woman to come with her.

44

EIGHTH V. The woman is either wounded or half mad with grief.

VARIOUS V. *(going toward the field)* Brunnhilde. Brunnhilde. What's happened?

(All return, accompanied by Brunnhilde leading and supporting Linda.)

BRUNNHILDE. *(urgently)* Help me now. I need a plane.

SIXTH V. What has happened? Your plane seems damaged.

BRUNNHILDE. I flew too low and ripped a wing on Hunding's horsemen.

VARIOUS V. *(all trying to talk at once)* Have you gone crazy? ...Were you trying to take part in that battle? You know our general orders forbid that.

BRUNNHILDE. *(impatiently)* I'll take my chances on that. But I've still more to do before father finds me. Take a look. Is he in sight?

VARIOUS V. Do you mean that Wotan is coming here? ... Then you really must be in trouble. ... He's never before come here to meet us. ... What can be so urgent?

BRUNNHILDE. *(hurriedly)* I haven't time to explain now, but he is coming. I want to get this woman out of Nibelung to the wilds and I need a plane.

FIFTH V. What threatens the woman?

BRUNNHILDE. *(resignedly)* I'll tell you quickly. This is Linda, mistress of Siegmund. I defied Wotan and did everything I could to turn the battle. It almost succeeded. If I could have kept Hunding confused for another hour, Siegmund might be alive yet, and his men fighting their guerrilla war, holed up in the capital. But Wotan guessed the strategy too quickly, and told Hunding I had no support. On my encouragement Siegmund fought and died in defeat. I must do what I can to save his mistress.

VARIOUS V. *(awestruck, and again all try to talk at once)* Brunnhilde!...You must have been mad!...You have disobeyed our foremost general order! ... What is the punishment? ... There are clouds; I can't be sure but I think a plane is coming. ... There's a break in the clouds just over the mountains. ... I believe he's coming on the horizon. ... No, the speck disappeared. ... Maybe it was a bird in the distance.

BRUNNHILDE. Linda must not be found here. Wotan would be treaty bound to deliver her over to Hunding. I must get her away or Hunding may find her. I should get her to the wilds, but my plane can't make it. Which of your planes could take one extra without removing the wounded?

SIXTH V. Are you going to involve us?

BRUNNHILDE. Ross, is your plane in the clear?

SEVENTH V. No. Hilda's is blocking it. Her's is in the best position.

BRUNNHILDE. Hilda, I'm taking yours.

EIGHTH V. Wotan would hold me guilty if I consented.

BRUNNHILDE. *(pauses for a moment's thought.)* I could take it without your consent. No. All of you would be expected to stop me. I can't involve any of you in my actions. But I must do something with her.

LINDA. Don't concern yourself about me. I have brought only death to my lover. The problem about what you are doing I don't understand, but there's no use touching others with the misfortune that follows me. I have nothing to live for and I don't want to live. It would be a kindness if you'd use your sword now to save me from a life that has lost all meaning.

BRUNNHILDE. *(takes time to put away the military problem and think of Linda.)* You and Siegmund can't die so easily. Siegmund still lives in the child you carry. Perhaps your baby is a son. And Siegmund would want him to live until he could die fighting.

LINDA. *(hesitates only a moment before answering.)* In my selfish hunger for death I had forgotten my obligation to life. You bring back to me the soul of Siegmund. For his deed and for yours, if it is possible, I'll have my baby, and if a son I'll rear a great warrior.

THIRD V. There's a plane on the horizon now. I'm sure.

SECOND V. Whatever you would do, do it quickly.

LINDA. I can try to live in the woods as Siegmund did when only a child.

BRUNNHILDE. *(decisively)* I'll take you to some home here in Nibelung where you can have your baby. My plane will be good for that much. Then I'll return and answer for my actions.

EIGHTH V. Hunding's men took a big defeat in a mountain pass near the valley. They've never come back for more.

BRUNNHILDE. That sounds like the best at the moment. Hunding will be busy for a month. And he will have longer licking his wounds.

THIRD V. Wotan will be in before you take off unless you hurry.

SECOND V. That plane flies as if fueled by venom!

BRUNNHILDE. *(to Linda)* Come then, quickly. We'll find you a home in the valley. No one there will betray you, and before Hunding comes you will have time to disguise yourself or find a way of hiding. And remember this always: while his child lives, a dead hero lives on forever. *(She takes a book and gives it to Linda.)* This looks like your diary. I saw it slip in a rock crevice while you were sleeping, and I looked for it again when I returned and found you. I suspect it has information that would be valuable to Hunding, but also to a hero who might reweld a weapon now in splinters.

LINDA. *(overjoyed)* Wonder of wonders! I have grieved for that almost as much as for Siegmund. If my negligence betrayed the names of those in the capital who stood ready to help I could never have had my own forgiveness. I searched about me madly, then thought Siegmund must have taken it. *(She goes willingly with Brunnhilde.)*

(They have barely had time to make the plane when Wotan's voice is heard from the landing field calling, "Brunnhilde! Stop!")

SECOND and THIRD V. Wotan landed just as she took off.

VARIOUS V. What can happen to her when she returns? ...Brunnhilde has courage but its greatest test will come today when she faces Wotan....What made her flout her general orders? ...I can't understand. ...Wotan is coming here instead of following her! ...I have never seen him as angry as this before.

WOTAN. *(comes on them stormily. He is wearing a long cape.)* Brunnhilde? Where has she gone? Have you given her assistance?

FIRST V. Can your rage be directed at us without accusation and hearing?

THIRD V. What have we done to bring on this storm of wrath?

WOTAN. Don't delay to gain time for whatever Brunnhilde's doing. If you've not already given her help, give her none now by tactics that delay. Answer me! Immediately!

FOURTH V. She brought with her a woman and planned to use our planes and our help to take her to hiding. Then she decided against it. We gave her no help.

SEVENTH V. Now she has gone to leave the woman elsewhere.

SIXTH V. But she will return.

WOTAN. That she would return I expected. So I didn't follow her when I landed. At least she has courage. ...But once I thought she had intelligence also. ...Seeing I was wrong about that I came prepared for any new found weakness. *(His wrath smolders in silence while the Valkyries move slowly back and watch with awe. He sits down then gets up and paces. He takes off his cape and sits again. He gets up and paces some more. Impatiently after a long silence he speaks half to them, half to himself.)* I have made a grievous error in entrusting missions to women. Women's emotions sway their judgment. ...But this time my own error of judgment has been disastrous. I gave my confidence to a daughter who was obligated to obey my orders. ...She was too close to me. She knew with what pain and grieving I uttered the words that I commanded her to obey. *(He pauses. There is a long silence that is heavy and ominous like a tangible thing.)* It was not enough that I had to

47

make a decision against myself, and against everything I hold dear, I also had to see my daughter defy that decision. She openly mocked me—as if I were a doddering old fool, uncertain of the heart I myself was forced to fetter. *(He is silent again, then addresses the Valkyries, still with passion but with more restraint).* By her actions she has brought shame on you and upon all the gods. Before our enemies she has cast into dust the ideals for which we lived and fought and died. She has counted as nothing honor and faithfulness to words spoken in solemn treaty. *(He sits down and broods. After a long while he leaps to his feet impatiently.)* Cowardice certainly she must not have, too! Why then does she not return and answer for her actions?

BRUNNHILDE. *(comes from the field and goes toward Wotan.)* Here I am father. Awaiting your sentence.

WOTAN. *(seems shocked by her sudden appearance. He looks at her in unbelief that she is unchanged. It is long before he speaks.)* I don't sentence you; your own action has shaped your doom for you. *(She does not speak. He waits. She stands silently. He is forced to go on.)* I awoke you to life and gave you my heritage. But now that you act for yourself I can not save you from the consequences of your action. *(He pauses, turns from her in thought, then looks at her again.)* As sovereigns we have become leaders of men's spirits, molding ideals and purifying purposes. Sometimes we became truly gods by heroic example. We inspired heroism amid darkness and confusion. We tried to raise men to honor by our own examples of honor. But we could take action only in the wilds. The Valkyries have been our only contact in Nibelung. As Chief of the Valkyries you were our proudest representative. But to your father you have chosen not to be a daughter. Honor you have chosen to replace with dishonor. While bearing the name Valkyrie you have chosen not to represent us. Of the gods you have chosen not to be one. Therefore, henceforth, you shall remain what you have chosen. You shall be yourself only—isolated and alone.

BRUNNHILDE. You cast me out and disown me? Is that the penalty?

WOTAN. Never again shall you lead the Valkyries. Never again shall you represent the gods. Never again shall you set foot in Valhalla. You cannot sit at the councils where matters of moment are being decided, nor join in the festive meetings where joy is celebrated as the soul of creation. From the god's company forever you are excluded, degraded and banned from your honored heritage. This because you have broken the faith that bound us by trampling our ideals in a moment's high emotion.

THE VALKYRIES. Brunnhilde! What hellish horror!

BRUNNHILDE. All you have given, you now recall?

WOTAN. You cannot claim the gods' aid and protection. Defenceless in Nibelung I must leave you. Alone, a woman beautiful and desirable, I am forced to leave you to Hunding and his horsemen.

VARIOUS VALKYRIES. No, Wotan! ... Please, reconsider. ... That sentence you must recall. ... The gods cannot fail to share the dishonor. ... All Valkyries will become objects of coarse jest and ridicule.

WOTAN. You have heard my decree. I know full well its horror and meaning. The shame, too, it brings to the gods I know well. The gods have one identity in the eyes of the vast public, a public that is unable to grasp our concept of individual sovereignty. The dishonor and shame of one is the dishonor and shame of all. This fate is the consequence of a broken treaty. Failure to accept the full reality, and pay the full penalty, would be the downfall of all honor. There can be no reconsideration.

(Brunnhilde sinks to a sad and thoughtful position on a broken pillar and the Valkyries, horror-stricken, recoil and draw back farther. Wotan speaks to them.)

WOTAN. As you fear her doom abandon the condemned one. Draw away from her now and speak to her never again. If any one should defy my order and furnish her help, that fool shall have the same fate. So heed my warning, you bold ones, take off at once and report back to Valhalla. Go! Save me the need for also pronouncing doom on your heads. *(They separate with muffled cries and hurry toward the field.)*

(Deepening twilight shows that night is closing in. Wotan and Brunnhilde remain behind alone. After a long silence she approaches him tentatively and gradually gains in confidence.)

BRUNNHILDE. Was my act so shameful that for it I should be so shamefully doomed? Was my offence so vile that for it I must suffer punishment so debasing? Was the dishonor of my deed so great as to rob me of honor forever? *(She sinks to a kneeling position.)* Oh, speak to me, father. Look at me. I don't ask for an unjust mercy, but make clear to me why you must cast out your child whom I know you love more than life.

WOTAN. Ask your deed and you can find but one answer.

BRUNNHILDE. Is there not a right that stands above treaty?

WOTAN. So long as men commit themselves by words, those words must be true.

BRUNNHILDE. The enemy breaks all the treaty but the hollowest form of its wording.

WOTAN. A man must be smaller than one behind whom he would hide. In questions of honor the gods must lead rather than follow.

BRUNNHILDE. Yet I knew only your mind ordered me and your

heart cried out against the order. Is the mind supreme and the heart not to be trusted?

WOTAN. *(sits on a broken column and looks at Brunnhilde.)* The heart is for loving. Reason is its strong guardian, and the guard must be ever steadfast in the battle against love's enemies. Our enemies must be destroyed not only with swords but with object lessons in honor.

BRUNNHILDE. My faith is in your wisdom not because I understand but because I love you. Perhaps being young I cannot yet understand the wisdom of your years. Or perhaps being woman I could never understand fully the soul of a man whose role in creation is selective destruction. I only knew that though you commanded against it, your heart yearned to aid those I would have aided.

WOTAN. Yet knowing my heart was fettered you refused to accept on yours the fetters with which I would so reluctantly bind it.

BRUNNHILDE. *(pauses to think what she will say then begins softly.)* I only saw that you were a being divided against himself, when I became of one piece and undivided. I know you have come up from the wilds and count as nothing men's crudity. You have always looked through their tatters into their eyes and seen their true worth. I have lived only in Valhalla and have come to think of sovereigns as superior, not only as they truly are — by comparison to those whose souls are mean and dwarfish — but also to others whose exterior mannerisms are merely a little less polished. There are differences in men truly, differences of soul quality, blood and breeding. But only today I learned what you always have known when sending us to recover the wounded: The highest men are not necessarily now in Valhalla. I am not only a Valkyrie; I am a woman and I have known a man's love; but I have never seen a higher man nor a higher woman than I saw in Siegmund and his Linda. And I have never seen a greater love than I saw in theirs. When I saw the sacrifice they made of themselves, and were prepared to make, to create in their unhappy world a place where love might freely blossom, then, before their feeble efforts, I was ashamed of the great power that the gods hold dormant. And so I chose to sacrifice my lover, myself, and if need be the honor of the gods to give the so little help on which their success depended.

WOTAN. You have done merely what I yearned always to do, what other considerations always restrained me from doing. But I am chief of the sovereigns, not merely myself, and have my first obligation to those who to me have sworn allegiance. We fought once for our very existence, even as Siegmund has fought, and charged as leader with the task of making decisions that will preserve the spirit and verity of that existence, I could not by my decisions stain the honor of a people born of honor. So my love for heroes, here defeated by my own treaties, I have had to hold like a burning fire imprisoned in my tortured heart. But you, seeing the vision of your personal heroism, have drunk with trembling rapture the emotional joy of following love's direction only, while I drank, in anguish, unmeasured woe, mixed with wormwood and gall. So your light-turned soul from now on must be your only guide. From me you are free. I must shun you and share no more with you my whispered thoughts — and the dearest wishes of my heart. No more are we father and daughter or gods together. As long as our days shall last I cannot again give you my greeting.

BRUNNHILDE. *(sees the effort he must make to keep his emotions from breaking him and tries to match his control with her own.)* I know I have been an unfit daughter and Valkyrie for the leader of the gods. Perhaps I am too much the daughter of my mother, who has refused to recognize what is not bred into blood and flesh and bone, for me to understand counsel that did not come straight from my own heart. My oath of allegiance to you was not the spoken words, but a faith in your being that gave me a will to love what you loved. An honor above that love was a slippery percept to hold in my woman's heart. But this much I perceive and ask you to forget not: The honor of the gods will suffer if I am made an object of scorn.

(Darkness has descended. Wotan kicks together some debris and lights a small fire. He takes his cape and puts it around Brunnhilde's shoulders as if to protect her, even while he is pronouncing sentence.)

WOTAN. To undisciplined love you have surrendered; undisciplined love must now be your master.

BRUNNHILDE. *(knowing what his words mean)* You know full well that while I have a sword or a precipice from which I can jump neither Hunding nor any other base braggart shall have me alive. But leave me my plane. A wing is damaged so it could not rise over the mountains. To make doubly sure, set the atomic fuse short so it cannot fly beyond this wilderness, and I'll wait here for the cowardly hordes' approach and let my plane's explosion satisfy a sovereign's concept of honor.

WOTAN. Your own fate is in you hands, but I cannot trick an enemy protected by treaty into sharing it with you.

BRUNNHILDE. Abandonment of a disabled atomic plane, I have always kept in mind, is permitted by treaty, provided it lies in an isolated area and full notice is given of its location, Give, then, that notice and let my plane be my death weapon when I need it.

WOTAN. *(has a brief respite from the pressure of his emotions by the necessity to think again as a military commander.)* That concession I can make if you wish it. Treaty requires only that I abandon you in Nibelung and give you no aid. I will set the fuse at its shortest running time, and you know the setting is not reversible, that you cannot fly beyond this uninhabited wilderness.

BRUNNHILDE. *(speaks with great care.)* Before I take your promise, let me explain and not trick you. If left unmolested — and cowards would not venture near — I might not start the motor. For myself life would be pointless, but the lieutenant who defied your order, who took off at my call and met death at your command, was my lover. He was love's hero and sacrifice. And under my loving heart I now bear his child. If I could I would give it life. I convinced myself of my duty when I talked to Linda in the same circumstance.

WOTAN. *(slowly and thoughtfully)* To make it possible for you to live here protected, does change the act's meaning.

BRUNNHILDE. If my child is a boy, he might serve your will here without your direction.

WOTAN. *(violently)* Don't try to flout honor and justice by appealing to emotions only, in a heart already wavering with its overburden of sorrow. With my heart cramped by its fetters and swelling to bursting, it is already difficult enough to make right decisions. I must act fairly, in spite of my emotions. On bare legalwording it could be decreed but the act must be fair also in its deepest intention.

BRUNNHILDE. What doom then shall I suffer?

WOTAN. Granting your request could be construed only as trickery. The plane would become a weapon, making this mountain a safe base of operation for all who would be sovereign, a base safe for them but protected always from massed enemy action.

BRUNNHILDE. *(again falls on her knees.)* Then forbid it also to the ones who follow the gods. Forbid it by *your own* decree conspicuously posted at evey access, side by side with the signs of Nibelung forbidding entry, and those giving notice of a live atomic explosive. This old castle was once an operation base and still has food and supplies sufficient for a hundred years of my needs. There is an old hermit couple on the mountain who could teach me to gather wild foods. Here I could wait until my son could fare forth for himself, or if a daughter she should wait until a hero brave and free should venture here to find her.

WOTAN. *(after a long pause to consider)* The intention holds to the treaty. It shall be as you wish.

BRUNNHILDE. *(clasps his knees as her tears flow.)* Father, I love you — even in your harsh justice. I know your suffering now and I know your years of suffering and remorse under the fetters of your treaties. Make of this act a monument that displays in full the fierce soul-consuming fire that lies in legality. Let "forbidden" signed by gods, and "forbidden" signed by giants, and "forbidden" signed by men be my guardian, so that if I bear a daughter she shall be claimed only by the truly brave and the truly free. Do not emphasize the dangers from my plane, lest those dangers tempt cowards who try to prove greatness with mere physical daring.

WOTAN. *(raises her to a place on a broken column, sits beside her on a higher projection, and places a hand on her shoulder.)* Your greatness and understanding I only know now when I must bid farewell to my valiant and glorious child. *(He repeats the word contemplating it painfully)* ...Farewell. ...Farewell. ...Farewell. ...Forever that word will echo in my heart. Never more can I give you love's greeting, never more ride with you by my side through the forest, or see your shining eyes at a banquet. This mountain top in the wilderness, holding the once laughing delight of my eyes, will burn forever in my heart. And, too, it shall be emblazoned before all men as the most highly forbidden spot on earth. Legality at last shall serve the purpose of the free. Legality's most terrible implication shall scare the timid, who, cowed, will not dare to come near. One only shall set you free, one freer than I, the god.

(Brunnhilde puts her arms around him. He holds her in a long embrace. Then he moves her head back and their deep searching gazes lock.) Those eyes so lovely and clear! Often in love I have kissed them, doing homage to your valor when, as a child, you lisped the praises of heroes. Those glorious radiant eyes! Often they have turned on me wide with anger as you heard the valiant restrained by reason's dictates when your soul decreed only a world radiant with joy. Still their gaze upon me is bright and radiant even as my lips imprint this last farewell! On some happier mortal may they yet look; this grief-stricken god they may gladden not again forever.

(He takes her head in both his hands.)

Now, heart-torn, I give you my last kiss and take your godhood away.

(He imprints a long kiss on her eyes and she sinks down by the fire. He moves slowly away toward the front and side. His receding draws into perspective the ruins of the damaged and deserted castle and the loneliness of the exiled figure by the camp fire. Pausing, he speaks his thoughts aloud without turning back toward Brunnhilde.)

Logi shall hear and aid me once more. As the legal reasoning of which he is master has made men false, so shall it build a wall that separates the false from the true. As it bound us who were called gods, so shall it bind all who are not greater than we.

(As he moves on his slowness must give time for the imagination to leap ahead to the projected spreading out of barbed-wire barricades and bureaucracy's formidable web. He pauses and voices his own picture of the coming realities.)

Forbidden signs in four languages will make a barbed-wire barricade into an impassible barrier for all who reverence words. On one side will be only Brunnhilde. On the other, walled together without distinction, will be dwarfs, men, and gods—the basest braggart and the one whom the gods called their chief.

(Grimly he absorbs the irony—and possible true significance—of the picture. His last words express his full knowledge that he must swallow the bitter whole.)

All who have traded truth for legality shall by legality be barred from the true.

(He restrains himself from looking back on the scene that will be imprinted on his mind forever.)

THE MORALITY OF THE EARLY NORTHERN EUROPEANS

THE MORALITY OF THE

EARLY NORTHERN EUROPEANS

by

John Harland

The central theme of Wagner's Ring operas is the central theme of the early Northern European "mythology" on which they are based. This theme is individual sovereignty versus group sovereignty.

The early Northern Europeans were caught between totalitarian groups encroaching on them from the Orient and from the Mediterranean area. They called these totalitarian groups giants or dragons.

Those originating in the Orient originated as dragons. They were formed by overt force and had to be met with overt force.

Those originating in the Mediterranean area were formed by surreptitious force and presented a semi-friendly front to confuse their enemies.

It is the attempts to deal with these tricky group sovereignty peoples that the "mythology" of the early Northern Europeans is concerned. The complexities of the conflict form the substance of the Ring operas.

Before approaching the morality of the early Northern Europeans, we need to translate their words and symbols into modern language.

"Giants" and "dragons" are readily understood as words for nations in which the innate sovereignty and integrity of all individuals had been wiped out. Giants and dragons were terms for the group entities that had to be dealt with as wholes.

The individuals who had been deprived of their individual integrity by subjection to brainwashing – and therefore had small, distorted souls – were called dwarfs. They had to be viewed and dealt with as individuals when detached from the giant or dragon. When so detached they were always attempting to form a giant or dragon of their own.

The Ring is the early Northern European term for the use of brainwashing, rather than overt force, to create a giant or dragon. Gorham, in his archetypal translation of Wagner's introductory opera "Das Rheingold," puts this description of the Ring into the words of Logi talking to Wotan:

"I have roved among all peoples to the ends of the earth and studied carefully their motivating desires and aspirations. The two prime movers in the drama of human destiny are love, born of the sexual heritage, and the will to power, born of organic being. By channelling both into a world of make believe, where they find a vicarious outlet in dreams on a television screen, the teras (monsters, a word used for both giants and dragons – bodies politic) gained control of the world and reduced its people to something less than human. Their civilization crystallized into its recognizable character when the power of mass opinion was admittedly made supreme, when politics became nothing but a TV program, and politicians became nothing but script writers and actors. The teras reached a dead end. The power of public opinion feeds on itself and destroys its own vitality. This fact was

58

acknowledged by the whimsical designer of the award for the best television program each year – the Ring in the form of a Uroborus, a snake swallowing its own tail."

Then Logi goes on to tell how Alberich, a dwarf, is going about refashioning the Ring in the wild lands – where Wotan, after two devastating atomic wars, is still trying to restore individual sovereignty. Logi says:

"With the example of the teras still before us, it would be thought that no one would again seek power by courting capricious public opinion.

"But already the Ring is being fashioned as it has been in the past – the natural wealth of the wilds is being transformed into manufactured articles. These made into status symbols produce the Ring in its original and crudest form. He who controls and manipulates their lure without scruple holds the power of the world."

Only a man who would forswear love, love of woman and love of the Rhinegold (the whole of nature) would fashion nature into status symbols that would enslave the human species. Wotan would not misuse the natural world in such a way. He was aware of the danger. He had already cautioned the Rhinemaidens, the uncorrupted maidens of the wild lands, to guard the Rhinegold.

Only one with a distorted, dwarfed soul would seek power by mutilating the natural world and denoucing love. Alberich has such a dwarfed soul.

Wotan would not mutilate the natural world to fashion the Ring. But, seeing the resultant power in action, he longed to possess the power. In an attempt to get the power Alberich wields, he captures Alberich.

Alberich had recognized the price to be paid for the Ring's power and accepted – with his eyes open – the curse that he knew went with it. Gorham makes clear the nature of the curse when Wotan seizes the power from Alberich. Alberich, made helpless, turns on Wotan with vehement seriousness and says:

"Having lost all else, I've got nothing left but my hate. But let me tell you something about visions in a night of hate. My hate gives me some dreams now, dreams of the god writhing in torment. I see visions now of your terrible downfall. That will be a downfall such as you can't even imagine. Do you know what will happen when you, a romantic idealist, begin trying to control and shape the thoughts and opinions of the whole vulgar populace? That, let me tell you, is something a lot different from leading people who follow you freely. That is something utterly outside the clean evolutionary process of a mutant surviving and helping others like himself to survive. That is the old Ring game. Do you hear me? The old Ring game! From this game no man can have joy. A curse rides with it forever. Even among the state officials of FASOLT and FAFNER, tired old men who have become nothing but figureheads, there is anguish and torment like you could never believe. Those in control are gnawed constantly by fearful envy and, in fact just as in symbol, they have found that the only reward for each coveted position is a self-devouring serpent. That alone should turn you away. But listen to this. The curse is in proportion to the stature of the Ring's holder! In the teras of our time the manipulators of public opinion have played only with pompous parades of their positions – and could lose only the coveted pomp. I – who am undoubtedly the master manipulator – have played only with power and could suffer only the loss of power. But you claim greatness and for you the curse will be great! You play with an ideal that to you is more than life, and so after losing it, still, in honor, you must live when life is less than worthless. The arrogant god I will yet see crawl. When you hold the Ring you will find youself committed to the ways

60

of a cringing coward – death–doomed but unable to welcome death." He laughs with malevolence then concludes, "Mark my words and start learning to walk with fear even now."

Wotan recognizes that the power of the Ring is the power to form a manipulated mass by brainwashing. He recognizes that the beginning of brainwashing is turning the Rhinegold (the natural world) into status symbols that everyone will covet. He recognizes that the widespread disdain for the sovereigns exists because the teras (the giants and dragons) have always had elaborately structured cities. Only two giants still remain after two devastating atomic wars, and they are mere fragments of their one-time grandeur as the world's leading nations. He makes a contract with these two, FASOLT and FAFNER, to build Valhalla, a city for the sovereigns, the "Men like gods."

It is an ambiguous contract worked out between Logi and the politicians of FASOLT and FAFNER. When it comes time for settlement, Wotan, who thought that he could use television broadcasts to counteract the broadcasts of the teras and teach the people of the world the virtues of individual sovereignty, balks at giving up the Ring.

Wagner's version has the spirit of Erda appearing to Wotan and advising him to yield the Ring. Erda is the wisdom of the past. Just as modern people talk of "the grim reaper" and picture death as a black robed skeleton with a scythe, the early Northern Europeans personalized the past, present, and future as three black robed women weaving the threads of destiny – Erda, Verdandi, and Skuld.

Gorham's version, which follows Wagner faithfully, has a real woman, a "child of the earth," giving Wotan the advice of historical wisdom. She says of the Ring, "All who covet the Ring become less than gods – and

61

less than men. Yield it, Wotan, yield it."

He questions her and concludes: "You speak a wisdom I once knew but had almost forgotten. In your words there rings a mystic might that I recognize. But hold a moment and answer this. Is all teaching wrong, even of truth?"

She, who was leaving, turns again and says, "Truth? A verbal truth that is grander and better articulated than organic reality? A truth for man that surpasses his blood and being? You have been warned. My words have said all that words can say. Weigh them wisely."

In the modern world the "mythological" Ring translates into status symbols and propaganda. The "magic" of the Ring is the "magic" of brainwashing.

Northern European "mythology" is not mythology at all. It is a clear statement of the intricate battles between a people committed to individual sovereignty and the manipulated masses that must be seen as group entities. Despite the clear statement of Julius Caesar that the people of Germania had not even heard of any of the multiple gods, there has been a fiction created that the Northern Europeans opposed Christianity with a religion of multiple gods. The Northern Europeans did not oppose Christianity; they opposed the totalitarian theocratic government of the medieval Roman Catholic Church. They had stories reciting the futility of their attempts to deal with group sovereignty people. Priests and patient monks, wanting to obscure the warnings implied by these stories, twisted them into stories dealing with superstitious magic – and called them "mythology."

While we are talking of mere differences in words and methods of expressing thoughts, it would be well to mention the Tarnhelm, even though it does not feature in the Valkyrie.

The Tarnhelm is the early Northern European term for the hidden power underlying a corrupted public ballot. It is the brainwashing that wipes out perception of the difference between individuals – that presents them all as equal, interchangeable units. It is the group–sovereignty concept of being a citizen, a statistic, instead of a person with individuality. It is the system of controlling people, who have been brainwashed to accept this concept, without exposing the manipulator behind the control.

As Wagner's Ring operas are put on the stage the Tarnhelm is a magic helmet that an individual can put on to make himself invisible, or allow him to assume whatever shape he chooses. Gorham translates the symbol into present day language. In both Wagner's and Gorham's version of the story, Siegfried, after destroying the one remaining dragon, unwittingly holds on to the Ring and the Tarnhelm for possible future use. Wotan covets the Ring only after it has been made by the dwarf who forswore love; he would disdain to use the Tarnhelm, which was a device used by the dwarfs to create the Ring.

Gorham makes clear what Alberich is doing when he pressures Mime to make the Tarnhelm for him. Alberich tells Mime to quit focusing on personalities. He says:

"You play up economics, play up high interest rates, play up minority issues, play up unemployment. Play up labor and industry conflicts. Give the dopes some harmless problems to think about. Get some voter petitions circulating. Let them forget whose running things. You concentrate on that old standard illusion that the voters are the boss. You bear down on that. It has always worked. Mr. Average Citizen is running things – MR. AVERAGE CITIZEN – the invisible man. And I am Mr. Average Citizen. I'm just a face in the crowd. You can't see me."

In a conversation with Logi, who has gone over to

63

the sovereigns, Alberich makes clear why Wotan will not use the Tarnhelm. He says:

"You, Logi, who walk with the sovereigns yet have colleagues throughout the world, think you are cunning and all men fools. But let me set you right. You sovereigns identify yourselves with your ideals, principles, codes of conduct, and concepts of honor. Then you must live for them and die for them – you can't compromise when the going gets rough. But I am identified with nothing. I can support or oppose any movement or any man, anywhere, as befits the moment. I have an invisible place under a banner of equality, fraternity, and the common good. I am just one of many, a common citizen. It is the people who rule, the people who make mistakes – and the people who get punished. But though you don't see me I am there, the invisible power – hidden, safe, fearing nothing. And I need not fear you and Wotan. Even if you sat in my chair, had title to all that I own, had my secret files and my contracts, you couldn't use them. You are prohibited by your foolish pride from pulling stings in the darkness. You want to stand boldly on a mountain top and let the full light shine on your glorious integration of beauty, noble ideals, and honor."

The Ring operas portray the many facets of the tricks used by the giants – or the dwarfs who manipulated the giants – and the strategy of sovereign individuals for dealing with these tricks – strategy that failed. The Ring operas – and the "mythology" on which they are based – appear to cover every trick of the group-sovereignty people. But apparently they did not.

Apparently theocracy was a form a giant could take that the Northern European "mythology" did not warn against.

Gaul was an area of Northern Europe that had fallen before a dragon – the Roman Empire. Gaul was obviously an example that stimulated consideration of

64

strategy for dealing with giants and dragons. The strategy for dealing with dragons usually worked. The Roman Empire, after lining up fully half of its vast legions along the Rhine and Danube rivers, was unable to penetrate the heartland of Northern Europe. The Roman Catholic Church instituted a theocracy by tricking Northern Europeans to kill Northern Europeans. That theocracy absorbed both the Roman Empire and the Northern Europeans' individual sovereignty culture – that for untold centuries had proved unconquerable.

When the inquisitions of the Roman Catholic Church had the people under full control, the priests and patient monks distorted the real points of conflict between the advocates of individual sovereignty and manipulated group entities into a religion opposing Christianity. It required the rare genius of Wagner to make a consistent story of them.

The difference between the modern use of the word "god" and the way it was used by the early Northern Europeans is the biggest obstacle to an intellectual understanding of the Ring operas. Wotan, called a "god," is obviously not a Northern European rival for a Mediterranean people's "god" when the word "god" is used to mean the Omnipotent Creator.

The early Northern Europeans viewed the whole of Nature – including all humans – as the Universal Creative Consciousness. Modern people who use the word "god" in a general sense – instead of referring to Jehovah, Allah, Krishna, et cetera – are using the word "god" to mean the Universal Creative Consciousness.

The early Northern Europeans used the word "god" to mean a flesh and blood person who demonstrated harmony with the Universal Creative Consciousness. A hero was one who fought valiantly against great odds. A hero could have any cause. A "god" was one in whose actions could be identified the long range direction of the Universal Creative Consciousness. It is a matter of word usage. Gorham bridges the gap by making it clear that his application of the term "god" to flesh and blood characters is based on a fictionalized television program called "Men Like Gods."

The difference in word usage is a big obstacle to modern people's understanding of the "mythology" underlying the Ring operas. However, after bridging the gap caused by misunderstood words and symbols, there is still a wide gulf before we arrive at full understanding.

There is no bridge across this gulf. On the other side, the early Northern Europeans had an utterly different morality from that which dominates the modern world. Their morality was implemented by a consciously created culture of individual sovereignty.

The culture of individual sovereignty – a conscious, emphatic, action–expressed yes–saying to the individual sovereignty manifest by Nature – was at the heart of their morality.

An attempt was made to recover this yes–saying to individual sovereignty by the people who broke away from the "old world" theocracy and formed the United States. The Declaration of Independence clearly articulates it and the Constitution of the United States fully implements it. As a formal heritage of peoples in the Western World, individual sovereignty still gets lip service. But, in the past two hundred years, commitment to it has seriously eroded – even in the United States. In modern thought, animal instinct and psychotic anarchy are called "individualism" – and "individualism" is dismissed as an impractical social concept. This leaves modern people with a moral vacuum. They give lip service to "individual freedom" – but communism, or any other plan for a one–world government, cannot be successfully opposed with a moral vacuum. Examining the morality of the early

Northern Europeans may help to fill in the vacuum.

The predominant modern morality is based on human words purportedly coming from a supernatural source. Those who merely reject a supernatural source – and go no further – are left to believe that unconscious matter accidentally created consciousness. This leaves them without any basis for morality. They can see that the "morality" purportedly coming from a supernatural source is in conflict with observable nature. Because it is the morality of the status quo, they give it lip-service acceptance. But they have no emphatic yes-saying to anything.

No perceptive person can deny that creative consciousness exists: It is conspicuously manifest in the human species. Those who are merely reacting to an obviously faulty "morality" – purportedly passed down in human words from a supernatural source – have come up with a tentative belief that matter came first and, by some accidental – and inconceivable – process, evolved into creative consciousness. This totally untenable thought process leaves morality to be synthesized. So modern humans are left with the choice between accepting a "morality" opposed to nature or synthesizing one from an untenable premise.

The thought pattern of the early Northern Europeans had no need for a supernatural. It was solidly grounded on perceivable realities. Everything visible and tangible was viewed as having evolved from a Universal Creative Consciousness. This included the sun, the moon, the stars, and the earth – as well as all living things. They viewed the purpose of consciousness in humans as determining the purpose of the Universal Creative Consciousness, and the purpose of human life as carrying on the purpose of the Universal Creative Consiousness. To them, everything WAS the Universal Creative Consciousness. To them, conflict between living things was nothing more than the Universal Creative Consciousness weighing and
67

evaluting its thoughts. Observing the natural world was the basis for learning the morality being continuously articulated by the Universal Creative Consciousness.

Gorham, in his interpretation of Wagner's "Siegfried," is faithful to the belief of the early Northern Europeans when he describes Brunnhilde's beliefs. He says that she has this view of the universe and the world:

ORGANIC LIFE

"When the creative intelligence was one, and the whole universe that was its thoughts had continued as a great galaxy of whirling stars for countless aeons, then the intelligence sought a new perspective for enjoying its past creations.

"Selecting an almost infinitesimally small speck on a long forgotten planet, circling a minor star, the aboriginal intelligence chose to look at the whole from this utterly small perspective. Leaving all past creations to continue as inertia, it identified with the speck and formed it into a cell wall, wherein the continuing will of all intelligence moved as life.

"The new living cell divided its self into two cells and found joy in the communion between life and life. Dividing into a greater number of cells increased the joy of the new creative venture even more.

"These cells absorbed the warmth from the star that was their sun; they drank the dew; they breathed the air; they swam in the liquid; they touched, felt, and explored the solids; they selected bits of the universe, and brought these bits into the new small spheres which were their living beings. They communicated with each other and perceived with joy their diversities as an adventure in infinite possibilities."

After describing the development of multicellular
68

organisms, the story goes on to talk about sex and the two lovers:

SEX

"Countless aeons of experiencing these organic thought realities, caused the creative intelligence within some organisms to perceive that life afforded two forms of joy: One came from creation by destroying and reworking what existed. The other joy was in perception of what already existed while cherishing its continued existence.

"Wanting to maintain balance between these two forms of joy, the creative intelligence within some cell-organisms evolved into two different sexes – one for the directional emphasis of each form of joy. One sex emphasized continuity of the existing; the other sex emphasized destruction of the existing in favor of a new creation; the union of the two became a condition necessary to any living creation of both."

LOVE AND DEATH

"Because the individual of one sex did not absorb an individual of the other, as happens in asexual enjoyment of other asexual life, a built-in limitation was needed. Death, as a corollary to birth, was therefore designed into all sexual entities as an essential condition of sexuality.

"Sex feeling for another living organism evolved into such full perception of the other – as an entity outside oneself – that it sometimes became love. The sexually-stimulated perception of an entity other than self also sometimes created love's corollary – a will to destroy when absorption was not the motivating impulse. Both were of equal value to the creative intelligence as a totality."

Note that joy of living was perceived as the prime mover of all creation, and perception of the meaning of sex led to perception of the meaning to be found in all of Nature.

The inquisitions of the Roman Catholic Church completely wiped out the articulated thought patterns of the early Northern Europeans. They have to be re-created by interpolating the original source from its two historically known tributaries – early Greece and early India.

In Greece the invading Northern Europeans gained full dominance and playfully compromised with the thought patterns of those brainwashed to believe in supernatural forces. The Greeks compromised by inventing a whole pantheon of gods. They did this as adults invent fairy stories for children. Their downfall came because they made another compromise. They mutilated their commitment to individual sovereignty when they compromised it to form a semi–group–entity run by a "scientific government." Despite these two compromises, the Greeks were carried for several centuries on the momentum of their past – their selective breeding for individual sovereignty. Because their past culture still colored their thoughts and actions, they never lost their joy of living. And so we look back on the historically known era before their downfall as "the Golden Age of Greece."

The opposite is true in India. The Northern Europeans pushing in from the north found dense populations that were committed to laws purportedly coming from supernatural gods. The Northern Europeans, trying to reach an understanding, attempted to explain the natural complimentary purposes of male and female in the native concepts by inventing supernatural gods as aids to explanations. They presented aborignal creative consciousness as one god, called Brahma, who then became two. These were Vishna, the god who created by cherishing and nourishing what was created, and Siva, the god who created by selective destruction. But the natives distorted the fictional

70

examples into supernatural dieties. And the population was so dense that the invaders never achieved domination. They withdrew unto themselves, meditated about the problem, found no joy in such existence, and, having a comprehensible idea of how the universe was created, turned their thoughts toward a method by which each individual could be "uncreated." That is, they sought for a method of reversing the process of creation and returning to the oneness of the aboriginal creative intelligence. Their stated objective, "Nirvana," means "blowing out, as of a candle."

The basic difference between them and the Northern Europeans was not primarily a difference in how they perceived the universe. It was being so overwhelmed by a dense incompatible population that they were unable to act. This brought on a difference in attitude - of saying "no" instead of saying "yes" to life.

Living is not meditation; living is action.

Morality is a code of action derived from a people's concept of the long range purpose of the Universal Creative Consciousness - and a decision to take action in harmony with that purpose.

The early Northern Europeans saw organic life as the thoughts of the Universal Creative Consciousness being weighed against each other. A clearly articulated individual integrity made an individual conspicuously recognizable as a significant thought of the Universal Creative Consciousness. He was to be loved and perpetuated as an individual, or opposed by an individual who considered himself to be a still more significant thought of the Universal Creative Consciousness. Individual sovereignty was axiomatic.

The axiom of individual sovereignty was derived from observation of Nature. There are herd animals but all mammals have a natural, biological commitment to individual sovereignty. Only some insects – ants, termites, and some species of bees – have a biological commitment to group sovereignty. And this can be seen as evolutionary regression: They had reached the plateau of sex and then mutilated sex to give the group sovereignty over its component individuals. They misused sex odors to do this.

Humans are included among the mammals who all have a biological commitment to individual sovereignty. But since long before the first histories were written, most humans began using words to do what the "social" insects did with sex odors. They used words to create cultures which overruled individual sovereignty.

The early Northern Europeans were caught between two man–made cultures committed to group sovereignty – one in the Orient and one in the Mediterranean area. The "morality" derived from these man–made cultures said to individual men "Thou shalt not kill" (EXCEPT on orders from a "constituted authority.") The "morality" derived from these man–made cultures said to woman, "You shall not have sexual relations and bear children except on authorization from a 'constituted authority'."

The early Northern Europeans countered these cultures with one that emphasized their observation of Nature. They formalized one–to–one individual combat in order to nip–in–the–bud any attempt of any man to form a manipulated group claiming group sovereignty. Among them, one–to–one individual combat had full social approval. In the same way social approval fully supported a woman's freedom to choose a mate without sanction or interference from any "constituted authority." The men viewed a woman's freedom of choice as that of a goddess; they viewed it as her individual articulation of the Universal Creative Consciousness.

Within the framework of accepted customs the

72

Northern Europeans could act – could actively assert their individual sovereignty with pride and courage. Their conviction that morality unquestionably backed the will and action of the individual gave an emotional power to individual will, which made "just living" into a joy that no people, ancient or modern, who are committed to a group sovereignty can ever know.

The Ring operas convey the emotional fullness with which the early Northern Europeans faced life.

Instinctively – responding to a biological heritage that predates brainwashing-to-accept-group-sovereignty – every perceptive person is caught up in the emotional power of Wagner's Ring operas. Every perceptive person identifies with Wotan, Siegfried, Brunnhilde and all the other characters who are valiantly, but tragically, opposing group sovereignty.

Gorham's stage plays, which translate the "mythological" archetypes into currently recognizable realities, lack, of course, the emotional power of Wagner's operas. But they remove the confusion waking consciousness has when forced to deal with dragons and magic as misunderstood symbols. The intellectual understanding that comes from these translations frees the emotions for full enjoyment of the operas without nagging intellectual questions. If we, the listener-viewers, embrace the yes-saying to individual sovereignty as a firm basis for morality, then we can vicariously experience the joyful actions of the various characters.

But, when leaving the operas to return to the present reality of a world dominated by group sovereignty, we know the despondency of Wotan.

The final facet of the early Northern European morality to be considered is this: They honored their freely given word to the death. Wotan was bound by self-imposed fetters.

Examining our feeling of despondency, we compare ourselves to Wotan, and we are exhilarated to discover that we are not bound by self imposed fetters. We do not have to drink Wotan's full cup of wormwood and gall. Our freedom to act is limited only by our ability to plan a feasible strategy of action. We examine the possibilities.

In one way we are in a better position than the early Northern Europeans. Their "mythology" was not full enough to include a specific warning against giants taking the form of a theocracy. The founders of the United States had learned about this form of giant, which was the one that destroyed their culture. They wrote into the First Amendment a constitutional prohibition against government by theocracy.

But we can still learn from the "mythology." A current condition is the same one that added to Wotan's despondency in the last scene of "The Valkyrie." Having freed ourselves from the fetters of a theocracy, we find dwarfs, men, and "gods" walled together without distinction. We are free to act but confusion stops our strategic planning.

Morality is a code of action and the Ring-forming dwarfs constantly present us with "some harmless problems to think about." They control the media and keep before everyone's eyes the choice between two "moralities" of which neither offers an acceptable code of action.

By our default, action is left to the dwarfs. In the last seventy-five years, they have made use of the Tarnhelm to re-fashion the Ring. They are just now beginning to move into full control.

The Ring loses its power if the machinations of the dwarfs are recognized and resisted. Recognition is the first necessity before devising a plan of action.

Wagner's operas are based on "mythology" that

74

was designed as a warning against conditions of the past.

Gorham's interpretation is set in the twenty-first century and fictionalizes atomic wars as a warning of what will happen if the dwarfs are allowed to gain full control. It has not happened yet. There is still time, if we act now.

If the men, and "gods" display to the whole world the culture of individual sovereignty proclaimed in the Declaration of Independence and implemented by the U. S. Constitution, the dwarfs will be crowded back into their dark hiding places. There does not have to be an atomic war. There does not have to be another Gotterdammerung – another downfall of the "gods."

SOVEREIGN PRESS

"Dedicated to Individual Sovereignty"

We proudly present

a representative sampling of our publications

SOVEREIGN PRESS, 326 Harris Road, Rochester, WA   98579   U.S.A.

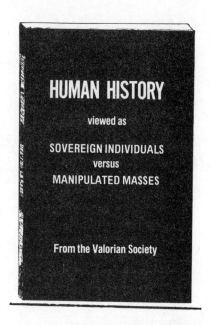

HUMAN HISTORY

viewed as

SOVEREIGN INDIVIDUALS
versus
MANIPULATED MASSES

From the Valorian Society

$4.00
paper
112 pages

86235   HUMAN HISTORY, Valorian Society

Humans are now poisoning the earth and manu-facturing weapons for atomic war. Only the social insects and humans engage in mass warfare.

This book shows that mass warfare goes against the long range direction of Nature in both cases. Mis-used sex odors brought on mass warfare among the social insects. Misused words brought on mass warfare among humans.

Beginning at a time before civilization, this book focuses on the conflict of two man-made cultures, the culture of manipulated masses and the culture of indi-vidual sovereignty. It views the Declaration of Inde-pendence and the U. S. Constitution – not as the beginning of "democracy" – but as a valiant attempt to re-establish the culture of individual sovereignty.

The struggle for survival of the human species is convincingly set forth as the struggle for survival between two man-made cultures. Misused words are the age-old weapons of mass warfare. A clearly stated human history is a counter weapon essential to sur-vival of the human species. This one has unexcelled clarity.

86235   5 x 8 permanent quality paperback $4.00

$5.00 paper
$9.00 hardcover
144 pages

79111 THE RING CYCLE. Melvin Gorham. This tense adventure story, dealing with violence, political corruption, the meaning of sex, and marriage versus no marriage has appeal for the reader with or without a Wagnerian background. By magnifying a point of contrast, it brings the Garden-of-Eden and the older Babylonian story of two lovers in a garden to the reader's mind for new examination. Brunnhilde's *Gottingarten* is a place entirely separated from the serpent and her Pagan pantheism knows joy as the soul of creation. This clear, powerful portrayal of the spirit permeating the Northern Europeans of prehistory opens the door on a whole new world where intellect and emotions are in full agreement.

79111	Hardcover	$8.95
79103 5¼ x 8¼ permanent quality paperback		$5.00

SOVEREIGN PRESS, 326 Harris Road, Rochester, WA   98579   U.S.A.

$5.00
paper
144 pages

84170 BRAVE NEW WORLD, A Different Projection. John Harland.

A rebel of the sixties generation has now matured and found words for his thoughts. In San Francisco John Harland, at nineteen, and an eighteen year old runaway, named Jill, joined forces to create a new world.

Along with his examination of various lifestyles he and Jill explored, he examines what's wrong with the establishment, with emphasis on manipulation by word conditioning, and looks at many well known doomsday books, such as Huxley's "Brave New World," Orwell's "Nineteen Eighty-four," and Zamyatin's "We." Harland may not be voicing the consensus thoughts of the sixties rebels but his world is startlingly new – and exclusively for the brave.   Suitable for classroom discussion.

Permanent quality 5 x 8 paperback $5.00

Recommended for library purchase by BOOKLIST. See full review in BOOKLIST 9-15-78.

Excerpt from newspaper review:
"As I predicted, the brighter lights of the rebellion of the sixties would only show their colors after the hubbub subsided."

                    – Burton Frye, REGIONAL NEWS, Lake Geneva, Wis.

$6.00
paper
208 pages

84197 CAMP 38. Jill von Konen.

This is the Jill of John Harland's "Brave New World." After several years of living in a "full dress rehearsal for a culture of individual sovereignty," and discussing with everyone involved the possibility of having a real, fully effective culture in the present world, Jill presents a detailed, fictional picture of such a possibility. This projection of the most desirable life everyone participating in the "dress rehearsal" could imagine turned out to be what every fragment left of their history points to as being the actual practices and ideals of the early Northern Europeans. The "dress rehearsal" people then realized that what they were considering was not the usual, wild dream, pie-in-the-sky utopia. Their dream world was actually a current model of Northern European lifestyle before "Christianity." So, without making an issue of the distinction between real Christianity and what was promoted by the Catholic Church, Jill gave "Camp 38" a subtitle calling attention to this fact.

Her invented story covers the detailed day-to-day life under an imaginary full scale culture of the sort visualized by the secluded Valorian Society groups. Strangely enough, this yearned-for Camp 38, which now has to be only a dream, could have been a state, fully supporting and supported by the United States Constitution. If the Constitution were still functioning and some Federal land were made available, Camp 38 could be a realized dream even now. It is an extremely interesting idea on which to orient.
Permanent quality 5 x 8 paperback $6.00

THE
PAGAN
BIBLE

$5.00
hardcover
296 pages

62012   THE PAGAN BIBLE.   Melvin Gorham.

"Pagan" originally designated one who would not conform to the state religion of Rome. Later the word was used to point out – in attempted derision – one who would not conform to any of the currently popular religions around the Mediterranean: Official Roman "Christianity," Judaism, and Mohammedanism.

Accepting the challenge implied in the historical meaning of the word, Gorham examines all major religions of the world from the Pagan perspective. The examination sears more often than it praises but the end result is not a barren waste. From the seeming ruin, the ghost of a Pagan, who has endured generations of cloyingly benevolent group rule, rises up in heroic stature to demand a new incarnation.

The work arranges known realities into a conceptual framework that appeals to one who says "I am," "I perceive," and "I will."   It shows that a fully conscious Pagan can find a way of life as far evolved beyond the institutional religions as the highest man is evolved beyond the most primitive organism of the Paleozoic slime. This is not a book for everyone, but the perceptive reader will arrive at a new plateau where a human individual has fully understandable meaning with relation to the total universe – and the total universe also has clear meaning.

Hardcover, 296 pages

$5.00

$5.00
paper
128 pages

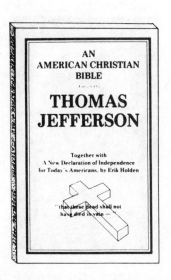

82146 AMERICAN CHRISTIAN BIBLE, extracted by Thomas Jefferson.

In 1904 Congress ordered the U. S. printing office to print 9,000 copies of the so-called Jefferson Bible for the use of Congress. These have largely disappeared and the work has been supressed. The reason for this is important to every American.

Jefferson, who wrote into the Declaration of Independence that governments derive their just powers from the governed, also wrote to Charles Thomson on January 9, 1816, "I am a real Christian." Seeking greatest Biblical accuracy, he compared Greek, Latin, French, and English versions and used scissors to cut away the theocratic injections that the 325 A. D. Council of Nice overlaid upon the teachings of Jesus. Theocratic Catholics and Jews have worked to suppress this Bible of a real Christian. Examination of Jefferson's views on Christianity draws attention to the fact that the Declaration of Independence, on which the United States was founded, clearly states rejection of theocracy.

This book contains a reproduced photocopy of Jefferson's work, along with an up-to-the-minute examination by Erik Holden of Christianity, biological development, and the all important relationship between religion, state, and individual sovereignty.

Permanent quality 5 x 8 paperback $5.00

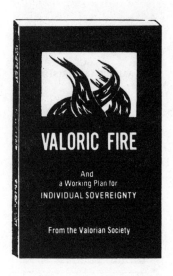

$5.00
paper
128 pages

84189 VALORIC FIRE and A WORKING PLAN FOR INDIVIDUAL SOVEREIGNTY. From the Valorian Society.

This unusual book first sets forth an imaginary campfire conference of people with varied pasts who are seeking to form a totally new human relationship based on a new morality. It presents a view of individualism and the prospect for social cooperation as it might appear after passing through the fire of compulsory groupism.

Then it presents actual excerpts from the published – and quickly withdrawn from circulation – book by the "Old Man" who formed the alternative society, described by John Harland's "Brave New World, A Different Projection." The excerpts include the exact wording for Agreements between Sovereign Individuals.

All who want to take part in any society or government seeking to be an alternative to the usual power structure of manipulated masses need to consider the ideas presented here. The facts and ideas here presented clarify the muddied ideological thoughts involved in most discussions of individualism versus "the greatest good for the greatest numbers."

Permanent quality paperback 5 x 8 $5.00

SOVEREIGN PRESS, 326 Harris Road, Rochester, WA   98579   U.S.A.

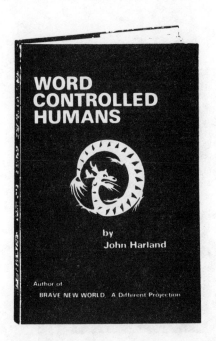

$5.00 paper
$9.00 hardcover
120 pages

81138 WORD CONTROLLED HUMANS, A Brief History. John Harland.

Brief and crystal clear, this would be an admirable basic work before any other history is studied in the schools. The two major conflicting concepts of how life should be lived are described as cultural directions that came into conflict before that conflict reached a climax in the teachings and crucifixion of Jesus. The Holy Roman Church's use of a false Christianity to promote a theocracy is sharply portrayed as the destroyer of both the teachings of Jesus and the Northern European cultural direction.

Then the American attempt to regain our cultural heritage of individual integrity is examined. The two hundred year long losing battle is covered from the perspective of religion, government, and money. Expanding to the worldwide scene, Harland looks at the errors made by the Germans under Hitler in trying to recover from the destructive effects of theocracy. He keeps his eye on what is significant rather than merely sensational.

This brief history puts the problems of the human species into a context where effecive action to correct them can be seen as a present possibility.

81138   Hardcover $9.00
8112X   5 x 8 permanent quality paperback $5.00

SOVEREIGN PRESS, 326 Harris Road, Rochester, WA   98579   U.S.A.

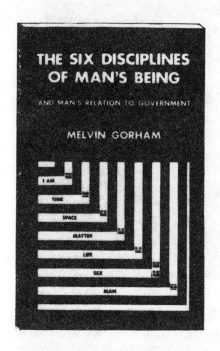

THE SIX DISCIPLINES OF MAN'S BEING

AND MAN'S RELATION TO GOVERNMENT

MELVIN GORHAM

$5.00

paper

128 pages

83162 THE SIX DISCIPLINES OF MAN'S BEING. Melvin Gorham. Gorham examines the life-direction pointed by evolutionary development and inherited memory with special attention to the meaning of sex. He carefully defines (1) Time (2) Space (3) Matter (4) Life (5) Sex (6) Man, and posits "an ultimate frame of reference" for total reality.

After looking with new eyes at reality unincumbered by cultural trimmings, he considers governments. Most governments are seen as surrogate parents that promote the anti-nature culture of mass manipulation. The history-old continuity of the oppressive practice suggests hopelessness. Then an opening is revealed which shows that a government can be the implement of all nature, and of nature's man, joined in one action. This is not a utopian dream of the future. It is a clear possibility and there is a plan for immediate action. 128 pages, paper $5.00

Excerpt from a review of **THE SIX DISCIPLINES OF MAN'S BEING and MAN'S RELATION TO GOVERNMENT**
"Melvin Gorham will be read and studied for centuries after today's bestseller authors have been buried with the people who found their books amusing."

— Burton Frye, RFD News, Belleview, Ohio

SOVEREIGN PRESS, 326 Harris Road, Rochester, WA   98579   U.S.A.

83154   THE FORCE UNDERLYING MASS WARFARE

This work sets forth the strategy of the Individual Sovereignty Society, ISS, for dealing with the causes behind the atomic bomb and all mass warfare – and for restoring Constitutional Government in the United States. Emphasis is on the unconstitutional power to control the value of U. S. money given to the Federal Reserve Bank, and the unconstitutional power of censorship given to those controlling radio and television broadcasting stations. Contains information about objectives, organization, and qualifications for membership in the ISS.

24 page brochure $1.00

84200   HUMAN CULTURE OF HUMANS , Valorian Society.

The focus is on the problem created by breeding for mass manipulation as it now exists in the United States – because the media is pushing our Government, despite our Constitution that opposes it, in the worldwide totalitarian direction. Bypassing the media that will not permit open discussion, this work presents a practical method for achieving its two immediate objectives: (1) Abolish the unconstitutional Federal Reserve System, and (2) Remove the unconstitutional "laws" that give the media power to censor open discussions and manipulate Congress. The necessary action to accomplish these objectives, which is already under way and rapidly accelerating, is precisely described.

32 page brochure $1.00

SOVEREIGN PRESS

Dedicated to Individual Sovereignty

Sovereign Press gives booksellers the usual discounts and credit terms, has widespread sales through wholesalers who buy for libraries, the academic community, and the few retail stores that order special books for good customers. But we are not geared to the usual mass promotion of "best sellers." Because most bookstores are now so geared, you cannot usually find our books in retail stores. To meet this condition we maintain full mail order facilities.

Individual orders are welcome.

Publisher pays postage
(including foreign) when payment is included with order.

Take 40 percent discount on 10 or more copies same title.

SOVEREIGN PRESS, 326 Harris Rd., Rochester, WA 98579 U.S.A.

ORDER FORM

To: SOVEREIGN PRESS, 326 Harris Rd., Rochester, WA 98579 U.S.A.

Publisher pays postage (including foreign) when payment in U. S. funds is enclosed with order. Take 40 percent discount on 10 or more copies of same title.

Quantity		Price	Extension
	American Christian Bible, Jefferson	5.00	
	Brave New World, Harland	5.00	
	Camp 38, von Konen	6.00	
	Force Underlying Mass Warfare	1.00	
	Human Culture of Humans	1.00	
	Human History, Valorian Society	4.00	
	Pagan Bible, Gorham hardcover	5.00	
	Ring Cycle, Gorham paper	5.00	
	Ring Cycle, Gorham hardcover	9.00	
	Six Disciplines, Gorham	5.00	
	Valoric Fire, Valorian Society	5.00	
	Word Controlled Humans, Harland p.	5.00	
	Word Controlled Humans hardcover	9.00	
	Sales Tax (Washington Residents)		
	Total (enclosed)		

Name _____

Address _____

_____ zip _____

ORDER FORM

Publisher pays postage
(including foreign) when payment is included with order.

Take 40 percent discount on 10 or more copies same title.

To:

SOVEREIGN PRESS, 326 Harris Rd., Rochester, WA 98579

Please send me the following: I enclose $ _____

Quantity	Title	Extension
	Sales tax (Washington residents)	
	Total	

Name _____

Address _____

_____zip _____